Sweet
SPEAK

TASTEFUL WORDS FOR CHRISTIAN GIRLS

Sweet SPEAK

TASTEFUL WORDS FOR CHRISTIAN GIRLS

Elizabeth Jimenez

GOSPEL
ADVOCATE
A TRUSTED NAME SINCE 1855

Published by Gospel Advocate Co.
1006 Elm Hill Pike, Nashville, TN 37210
www.gospeladvocate.com

ISBN: 978-0-89225-658-7

DEDICATION

Dedicated to my girls class in Mexico for inspiring me
to write the book in the first place, to my parents, for always
encouraging me and instilling confidence in me,
and to my husband, José Luis, for supporting me through
thick and thin as I juggle family, career and now
my dream of writing.

Table of
CONTENTS

❧ INTRODUCTION ❧

*P*owerful. Deceitful. Vicious. Uncontrollable. Intimidating. Untamed. Ruthless. Cunning. These are just a few of the many words we could use to describe the tongue. Think back to a time when your tongue got you into trouble. Was it a lie you told? Gossip? Profane language? Nearly all of us have said something we're not proud of. Unfortunately, once the words left our mouths, there was no way to take them back.

God understands how difficult it is for us to control our tongues, which is why the Bible is full of verses on the subject. Take a minute to read James 3 and answer the questions that follow.

What three things did James compare the tongue to in James 3:3-6?
1.

2.

3.

According to James 3:8, what can no man tame?

According to James 3:9, what two actions do we do with our tongues?
1.

2.

According to James 3:13, 17, who is considered a wise person?

Just as a small bit controls a horse (James 3:3) and a "very small rudder" controls a ship (v. 4), our tongues control our every action. "Even so the tongue is a little member and boasts great things. See how great a forest a little fire kindles!" (v. 5). No doubt the tongue is one of the most important, although one of the smallest, parts of our bodies. Just think about everything we do with our tongues: we eat, drink, taste, talk on the phone, shout, sing, pray, encourage, tell others about Jesus and much more. However, we also use our tongues in ways no Christian should feel proud of. Criticizing, boasting, denying or betraying others, talking about friends behind their backs, gossiping and lying are some examples. For these ungodly actions, James referred to the tongue as "an unruly evil, full of deadly poison" (v. 8).

Throughout this book, we will discuss some of the purposes of the tongue and how we, as young Christian women, can control what comes out of our mouths. The tongue is like a fire (James 3:5). Why? Left uncontrolled, our poor choices of words spread to others as quickly as a fire touches other trees. We can burn others by our bad influence. It could be a single lie, a single bad joke, even a single bad word – but if we do nothing to control our tongues, undoubtedly others will be hurt and further destruction will spread. A forest fire starts with a single branch on fire. It starts slowly, but little by little, the other trees begin to burn until eventually the forest is no more. The tongue is small, but incredibly powerful.

James also said, "Does a spring send forth fresh water and bitter from the same opening?" (James 3:11). In other words, our words should be completely sweet – not half sweet and half mean. Imagine drinking sweet tea or ice-cold lemonade with salt poured into it. You will likely spit it out as soon as possible. Just as our drinks are not meant to be sweet and salty at the same time, neither should our speech. Our words should be clean and pure at all times, never mixed with the filthiness of lies and gossip. Otherwise, we can be viewed as hypocrites, not as true Christian examples. Which would you rather be: salty or sweet?

> "If anyone among you thinks he is religious, and does not bridle his tongue but deceives his own heart, this one's religion is useless" (James 1:26).

As you read this book, think about how you use your tongue – whether good or bad – and how you can control it to be a spring of sweet water that others draw near to rather than a consuming fire that turns others in the wrong direction. Don't be one of those people who talks one way around coaches, teachers and people at church but a completely different way around friends, teammates and classmates. Be someone who says the right thing all the time.

In the space below, write three goals you have for your tongue that you hope to accomplish by the time you finish this study.

1.

2.

3.

How to Use This Book

This book can be used in small groups or individually.

1. In the Classroom. If you are using it as a class or small group, please encourage the girls to share examples of how they have used their tongues for good and bad. You will notice questions throughout the book that will help spur these conversations. If you'd like, the girls may answer the questions as homework so that they are more prepared to talk in class.

Additionally, you will find "Practice What You Speak" sections in each chapter, which include group and individual activities. The group activities should take place at the end of class, with as many of the girls participating as possible. The individual challenges are for anyone using the book. The challenges are for them to apply what they have learned from the book, so they should do this at home on their own time. However, group leaders may choose to open each class by asking girls to share if they completed the individual challenge and, if so, what the results were.

2. For Personal Study. If you are reading the book for personal Bible study, you may also use the questions to reflect on what you have done in the past and what you can improve in the future. Make sure you set aside a certain amount of time. Try to do it in a comfortable place at the same time every day. And remember, it takes 21 days to develop a new habit, but it only takes one to start.

PART 1

Sweet, Delicious
WORDS

ENCOURAGE, PART 1

Miranda was a 5-year-old girl who loved drawing pictures so much that she devoted every minute to creating beautiful new images for her mother and father. Every Christmas and every birthday, all she wanted was new crayons, colored pencils or drawing pads. One day she decided to make a special picture for her favorite uncle.

"Look!" she exclaimed when she finally finished. "Do you like it?"

"What is it?" the uncle responded.

"A horse."

Her uncle, forgetting for a minute that he was talking to a 5-year-old, foolishly asked: "A horse? It certainly doesn't look like a horse."

He immediately realized his mistake, but it was already too late. The little girl's eyes welled up with tears, and despite the uncle's apology and pleading, she could not be persuaded to make another picture. Later, when Miranda was in high school and teachers asked her to draw a picture, she would automatically respond: "Someone else can draw it. I'm not a good artist, and I don't like drawing much anyway."

Miranda felt so insulted by her uncle's rash comment that she immediately changed her mind about her drawing ability – and herself. Insults hurt. Sometimes they are just as hurtful as someone calling us a bad word to our faces; sometimes words hurt so badly that we change our perception of ourselves and lose confidence in ourselves.

{ *"Anxiety in the heart of man causes depression, but a good word makes it glad"* *(Proverbs 12:25).* }

All of us know what it feels like to get our feelings hurt. I can still remember when I stood in my friend Ashley's backyard eager for another day of tag and bike-riding when she suddenly said, "I don't want to be your friend anymore." Although I was only 6 years old at the time, the words stung like darts. Think back to a time when someone insulted you. Were you surprised afterward? Angry? Sorrowful? Chances are you can remember exactly what the person said to you and exactly how you felt afterward.

According to Proverbs 18:21, "Death and life are in the power of the tongue, and those who love it will eat its fruit."

1. What do you think the first part of this verse means?

2. What do you think the second part of this verse means?

We can use our tongues to build up, or we can use our tongues to tear down. The damaging effects of an insult tend to last far longer than the juicy tenderness of a compliment. Because we all understand how harmful insults can be, we need to be especially careful not to make fun of others. Instead, we should constantly try to build up and encourage with our words.

The Importance of Encouraging Words

Do You Speak With Kind Words?

The Bible emphasizes over and over the importance of kind words. First Corinthians 13:1 says, "Though I speak with the tongues of men and of angels, but have not love, I have become sounding brass or a clanging cymbal." What does this verse mean to you? To me it means that if we don't speak with love, our words mean nothing. Ephesians 4:29-31 says:

> Let no corrupt word proceed out of your mouth, but what is good for necessary edification, that it may impart grace to the hearers. And do not grieve the Holy Spirit of God, by whom you were sealed for the day of redemption. Let all bitterness, wrath, anger, clamor, and evil speaking be put away from you, with all malice.

Are your words full of love and "good for necessary edification"? Here are a few guidelines you can use to find out:

- You don't just wait for opportunities to come along when you can encourage someone with your words; you seek them out.

- Your words are pure and clean – the kind of words that other Christians would not be ashamed to hear.

- You don't like to talk about anyone unless it's something pleasant.

Unfortunately, very few of us could claim to meet all three guidelines. Anytime we are about to open our mouths, we first need to consider whether our words will be edifying to those who hear them. Most of us have heard our moms say, "If you can't say something nice, don't say anything at all." That old adage is still true, and it's the same idea presented in Ephesians 4. If our words are not going to build up and encourage those around us, then they're not worth saying. Would you want to be the cause of a great conflict or argument simply because you failed to think before you spoke?

Do You Seek Out Others to Encourage?

Be honest with yourself. Do you use your tongue to encourage others any time an opportunity presents itself? Most of us would have to say no. Saying a kind word seems simple. Yet so often we allow the busyness of our daily lives to overshadow the needs of those around us. Instead of searching for the people who need encouragement the most, we prefer to socialize only with our closest group of friends or to leave church or school as soon as it's over – before we have time to talk to anyone else. How hard is it, really, to tell someone who is suffering that we're praying for him or to tell a friend that we have missed seeing her at church services and youth events? It's really quite simple and only takes a few seconds. Even the shyest girls can send thoughtful notes or share their beautiful smiles. There are no excuses for failing to encourage others.

> **Edify (verb):**
> to teach (someone) in a way that improves the mind or character [1]

17

Whom Should We Encourage?

Our Family Members

For many of us, our family members know us, love us and support us more than anyone else. Therefore, we owe it to them to use as many kind and encouraging words as possible. Yet we consistently fail to pepper them with the praise, gratitude and consideration they so richly deserve. How often do we choose to take out our anger on them rather than calmly explain the source of the problem? How often do we prefer to share personal, special details of our lives with our friends and classmates more than with our parents and siblings? How often do we thank our parents for all they do for us? Show love for your family every day by refraining your tongue from harmful comments.

 List at least one kind thing you could say
to the following family members.

Mother: _____

Father: _____

Sister: _____

Brother:_____

Grandmother: _____

Grandfather: _____

Why do you think we often struggle to use kind words
with those we see the most, like our parents and siblings?

_____

_____

_____

Our Brothers and Sisters in Christ

Just as with our physical families, we also need to encourage our spiritual families. Provided are some examples of situations when you might need to encourage a fellow Christian. Take a minute to write some simple words or phrases you can use to show encouragement in each situation. Remember: write only what you would *say* in each situation, not what you would do.

1. Your friend has not been at church for the last two weeks, and you don't know why.

2. The young men of the congregation have just finished leading the worship service.

3. A young married couple plans to live in another country as missionaries for the next five years.

4. An older man who has been studying the Bible was just baptized.

5. A girl a few years older than you came forward asking for forgiveness for sins she has committed.

6. Your youth minister is discouraged and thinking about looking for another job that is not church-related.

We should show kindness and love to everyone with the words we use, but especially to our brothers and sisters in Christ. So often Christians refuse to speak to one another just because one person decided to argue and bicker with anger rather than encourage and edify with love. Some churches even split because of harsh words, and some Christians hold grudges for years or stop coming to church altogether for something as silly as a comment about their appearance. How terrible it would be to cause a fellow brother or sister to stumble because of one unnecessary comment we made! Even though we will never agree with everyone, we should show love to our brothers and sisters at all times, starting with the words we use.

Our Non-Christian Friends and Acquaintances

Sometimes it's easier to encourage our brothers and sisters in Christ because we see them more, know them better and don't have to worry as much about their reactions. Encouraging them comes naturally because they are like our family. Those who are not yet part of Christ's family may be harder to encourage because we don't always understand their situation, but many times they need the most encouragement. They may have more pains, more struggles, more burdens. We have a great responsibility to show them Christ's love in those difficult times.

→ Write what you would say to some non-Christians in these situations.

1. Your friend from school is worried that her parents will get a divorce.

_____

_____

2. Some students at your school lost their homes and belongings after a recent tornado.

_____

_____

3. A boy in your class gets made fun of a lot because he sometimes smells bad and wears the same clothes over and over again.

_____

_____

4. Someone broke into your coach's house while he was on vacation and stole a lot of money and valuable possessions.

_____

_____

5. A girl in your grade that you don't know very well always sits by herself at lunch.

_____

_____

6. Your favorite teacher's dad just passed away.

_____

_____

Those We Don't Know

Which of the situations listed previously was easiest for you think of an answer? Which was hardest? If you're like me, the easiest to encourage are the people who are closest to you, like friends and family, and the hardest to encourage are the people you don't know at all. Yet God sent His only Son for the entire world (John 3:16), and He expects us to love and reach out even to those we don't know.

Jesus demonstrated this principle perfectly in John 4 when He talked to the Samaritan woman. "And at this point His disciples came, and they marveled that He talked with a woman" (John 4:27). Remember that in this time period, it was not common for people to make friends with those living in other areas, such as the Jews with the Samaritans. For Jesus, there were no boundaries of race or color, and there shouldn't be for us either.

Think about all the people at work and at school who have no friends or who constantly get made fun of. We could just go along with the crowd and ignore them or even talk badly about them, or we could be like Jesus and reach out to them with kind words. Sometimes a simple "hello" is all it takes to turn a person's bad day into a good day. By doing so, we will set the right example for others, just as Jesus did for His disciples. At first, the disciples were shocked that Jesus would talk to a Samaritan woman, but Jesus was unlike anyone they had ever known.

What Not to Do: Zophar

One example of a non-encouraging person in the Bible is Job's friend Zophar. Remember that Job had just lost everything except his wife because the devil decided to test his faithfulness (Job 1–2). Read Job 11:1-6, 13-20, and answer the questions that follow.

1. How were Zophar's words discouraging?

2. What did Zophar want God to do?

3. What do you think Zophar meant when he said "God exacts from you less than your iniquity deserves" (Job 11:6)?

4. What is another word for iniquity?

5. What did Zophar think Job should do?

6. What did Zophar think was the cause of Job's suffering?

7. What are more encouraging words that Zophar could have said to Job?

Zophar urged Job to repent and insisted that the only reason he was experiencing so much tragedy was because of his wickedness. Even though it's always correct to repent when we do something wrong, this was not the right thing to tell Job because we know he had committed no wickedness (Job 1:1-5).

Think about Job's wife. Job's wife certainly did not support her husband as the virtuous woman of Proverbs would have. Proverbs 31:26 says, "She opens her mouth with wisdom, and on her tongue is the law of kindness." Instead, she told Job: " 'Do you still hold fast to your integrity? Curse God and die!' Job answered her, 'You speak as one of the foolish women speaks. Shall we indeed accept good from God, and shall we not accept adversity?' In all this Job did not sin with his lips" (Job 2:9-10).

> *"The best exercise is bending down to lift someone else up!"*
> *— Unknown*

The virtuous woman of Proverbs sets a standard for us to follow. Can you say that you open your mouth with wisdom? Can you say that others look up to you because of the words you use? If not, strive to have wiser, kinder speech every day. Think of girls or women you know who demonstrate "the law of kindness" in their speech. On the other hand, think of ladies who are more like Job's wife or his friend Zophar and are not very kind or encouraging. If you are not up to caliber with the virtuous woman yet, then you know whom you can imitate to be more like her and whom you should avoid listening to. You can't always control your family, but if you find that some of your friends are negative in their speech, then you may need to choose different friends to spend your time with.

 Here are some simple phrases you can say to encourage others:
"Well done."   "Thank you."   "God loves you."

Can you think of any others? _____

_____

_____

A Time to Build Them Up

In this chapter, we discussed some ways we can encourage others with kind words, and you wrote some things you can say in different scenarios. Now think of three people you know who need encouragement right now. It can be anyone — someone from school, a man on the street, your grandmother, your grandmother's aunt, anyone. Write the names of the three people and what you will say to encourage each one.

Name: _____

Encouraging Words: _____

_____

Name: _____

Encouraging Words: _____

_____

Name: _____

Encouraging Words: _____

_____

When you see these people again, don't forget to use your tongue to build them up.

Practice What You Speak
Individual Challenge: Phone Call

 ## Purpose:

To experience how easy it is to encourage others, even when we don't know them very well.

 ## Instructions:

Review the prayer list at church. Look for one person on the list you don't know very well, and ask the church secretary for the person's phone number if you don't already have it. Then call the person and offer words of encouragement. Obviously the words you choose will depend on the person's situation, but remember, it can be something as simple as "Hi, my name is _____. I go to church with you. I just wanted to let you know I'm very sorry about your situation, and I'll be praying for you."

Chapter 2

ENCOURAGE, PART 2

I played a lot of sports when I was younger, and I had a variety of coaches. Some were extremely competitive, so during games they would yell at the top of their lungs, "Get the ball!" "Don't do that!" "You have got to do better!" or a number of other words that sometimes felt more like threats than encouragement. I can particularly remember the father of one of my teammates rising quickly from the bleachers, flailing his arms frantically, and rebuking me, all because of one tiny mistake I made.

On the other hand, with some of my other coaches, I knew from day one that they cared more about each and every girl on the team than about winning. These coaches would choose genuine words like, "You all did your best today," "Nice try," or "I am so proud of you!" – for every practice, every game, every victory, every defeat. They told us just what we needed to hear at just the right time, and our team naturally followed their examples. Even on the days we lost, we would leave with smiles on our faces, pleased with our efforts, and motivated by the team camaraderie.

Now that we understand who we need to encourage, let's talk about how we can encourage them. There are people suffering all around us, and we have the power to help them in their suffering with our words of support. But we must choose our words carefully and realize that a few nice words may not make them feel any differently. Speaking with encouragement requires thought, love and tact. We cannot just say anything we want. We must first think about what that particular person needs in that particular situation, and then we must choose the right words to have a lasting, positive effect.

> *"Spoken words can't be erased. Don't blurt what might hurt."*
> *— Unknown*

How Can I Be Encouraging?

Think Before You Speak

To have a positive effect on others, we need to think before we speak. If we simply blurt out the first words that pop into our heads, the words may not sound as sweet – even if we have good intentions. On the other hand, if we think before we speak and plan to use thoughtful words, we may be able to help someone bounce back from discouragement, anger or heartache. Here are three questions to ask ourselves before we speak.

1. What would Jesus say in this situation?

If we try to model our words after the greatest Man who ever lived, it is highly doubtful that we will fail. Jesus did not show partiality of persons, and we need to imitate His example of speaking loving words to everyone – no matter what they look like or where they come from.

2. What does this person need right now?

Before we say anything, we should first identify what the person is struggling with and what we can do to help. Although there are multiple kind and encouraging phrases we can use, not all of them are appropriate for each situation.

Ecclesiastes 3:7 says there is "a time to keep silence, and a time to speak." Sometimes what the person needs is not for you to say anything but for you just to be there by his or her side. Then, when the time is right, you can offer encouraging words. This is especially wise when you aren't sure what to say. Maybe you've never experienced what that person is going through. It is often wiser to keep silent than to say something that could bother the person more.

A friend of mine once burst into tears after receiving tragic news about her family. Noticing her distress, an acquaintance rushed to her side and just patiently sat with her and rubbed her back. The acquaintance didn't know why she was crying and especially didn't know what to say, but just having her there was enough to bring comfort. Even though these two girls didn't know each other very well at the time, they became great friends – all because one responded quickly to the other person's need and didn't worsen the situation by trying to talk about it.

Although we cannot entirely understand what another person is going through, we need to do our best to understand that person's needs, sympathize with her, and provide the most appropriate words of help when the time is right.

Read Job 2.
What did Job's three friends do at first to comfort him?
Why do you think it's often wiser not to say anything when someone is suffering?

_____

_____

_____

_____

3. How will this person react?

Not everyone will react to our words in the same way. Differing character traits and personalities can play a big role in whether our words are encouraging or just plain silly. Even when we say something we ourselves believe is encouraging, the hearer could misunderstand us or think that we are just being critical.

For example, a father trying to motivate his son before a little league game might say, "Don't play bad today, Son." The father thinks he has just said something to prepare his son for the big game. The son, however, could have one of two reactions, depending on his personality:

(A) He knows his father is only trying to encourage him to do his best and understands that what his dad meant was "play well."

(B) He immediately starts thinking: "Why would he say that? Do I normally play bad? He thinks I'm a bad baseball player."

Think before you speak, and try not to say anything that could be misunderstood as something negative.

Elizabeth Jimenez

 In Hebrew, which was the language used to write the Old Testament, there are at least three ways to say goodbye:

- Shalom (shah-lohm): peace
- Kol Tuv (kohl toov): be well
- L'hitraot (leh-hee-trah-oht): see you soon [2]

How many different ways can you think of to say goodbye in English?

_____

_____

_____

_____

Give an Invitation

In chapter 1, we learned that we should encourage everyone – including those who are struggling, feel depressed, or don't have a lot of friends. One way to encourage people in these situations is to invite them to go somewhere or do something; it also wouldn't hurt to add something like "I hope you can make it." It could be an upcoming party, a celebration, a church event or just a trip to the movies with you and your friends. I know some people who refuse to attend any kind of event unless someone invites them personally. If someone just mouths the words to them one time, they instantly feel better and are much more likely to go. If not, they begin to feel rejected, depressed and unaccepted.

When I was in college, I hosted a cosmetics party, and many of my friends canceled at the last minute. We needed at least five people for the party to be worthwhile, so I frantically walked down the dorm hallway, knocking on doors and asking people to come. The last room I came to belonged to a girl who lived by herself and stayed in her room all the time with her door closed. Naturally, I felt a little awkward inviting someone I barely knew, but her face instantly lit up when I told her – and I provided her with the opportunity to interact with other girls. The last person I would have expected to come to the party was the quickest to say yes.

Oftentimes the people who withdraw themselves the most are the ones most in need of an invitation. And you never know what kind of positive results extending an invitation will bring – maybe even a new friendship. Why risk causing someone to feel even more hurt and depressed just because you didn't take the time to give them one invitation?

The Examples of Ruth and Naomi

You may already know the inspiring story of Ruth and her mother-in-law, Naomi. But we are going to examine the story again, focusing on the encouraging words Ruth and Naomi used. Read Ruth 1:1-17. The sections that follow show some of the lessons we can learn from this amazing story, all of which give us additional ideas on how to encourage others.

Don't Forget to Say Goodbye

When terrorists hijacked airplanes on Sept. 11, 2001, many of the men and women aboard started calling home to tell their family members "I love you." Many of them didn't say "I love you" as they left the house that morning, and they wanted to make sure their families heard these words before they died. If you had been one of the people on the plane that day, would you have had to call your family to make sure they knew you loved them? Or would your friends and family members have already known by the way you tell them goodbye each day?

In Ruth 1:8-9, we can see that Naomi did more than just tell her daughters-in-law "goodbye." She obviously loved and cared for the two women very much. Notice the encouragement in these words: "The LORD deal kindly with you, as you have dealt with the dead and with me. The LORD grant that you may find rest, each in the house of her husband" (vv. 8-9). Rather than just saying, "See you later," giving them a quick hug, and going on her way, she took the time to pay tribute to her daughters-in-law.

Do you ever think about the words you use to say goodbye? So often we become so focused on our personal lives that we forget to say goodbye altogether, even to the people we care about the most; or maybe we say goodbye, but not in a meaningful way. For example, we yell "Mom, I'm going shopping!" as we're heading out the door. We say a general "See you later" to a group of friends at church rather than saying something to each of them personally. We feel so excited on the last day of school that it never even crosses our minds to say: "Have a good summer, Mrs. So-and-So. Thanks for everything you taught me this year."

You never know when you will see these people again, so why not give them a goodbye every time you see them that lets them know they hold a special place in your heart?

Record some meaningful ways to say goodbye to this list of people.

Parents: _____

Best Friend: _____

Classmate: _____

Youth Group Member: _____

> *"Keep your words soft and sweet in case*
> *you need to eat them." — Unknown*

Offer Compliments and Blessings

We also find praise in Naomi's words to her daughters-in-law. Record the compliment she paid her daughters-in-law as she was departing from them:

_____

_____

_____

A sincere compliment will not soon be forgotten. Most of us can probably still remember the exact words some of our elementary teachers used to compliment us or the boys we had a crush on or even people we don't know. Many of my former teachers encouraged me to become a writer. Who knows, maybe I wouldn't have had the confidence to write this book if not for their kind words.

A compliment could be something as simple as "Your haircut looks really nice," or something more expressive, such as "I really admire how you handled that situation in class today." Whatever the case, others will be more likely to remember us and think more highly of us if we praise them from time to time. We won't just be another face in the crowd or another person they talked to but can't seem to remember when or why. We will be a friend. In addition, compliments will go a long way in boosting others' confidence and motivating others to pursue their special jobs and talents.

Besides praising them, Naomi offered her blessings upon the two women. She hoped they would have fulfilling, prosperous lives. When was the last time you wished God's blessings upon someone? Saying "God bless you" or telling someone that you will be praying for him or her are two more ways we can say goodbye with style.

Speak Lovingly and Selflessly

Write Ruth's words from 1:16:

_____

_____

_____

Although we don't know much about Ruth's character, we can speculate from these words that she was a very loving and devoted person. Wouldn't you like for someone to consider you selfless and loving just by hearing you speak one time? Ruth's example is one of several we will be studying that shows us how easily our speech can influence our reputations.

By choosing to care for her mother-in-law rather than tend to her personal needs or desires, Ruth acted very selflessly. She was probably a beautiful young woman who could have lived just about anywhere she wanted, but instead she chose to stay with her mother-in-law. It's not easy to follow someone wherever he or she goes – least of all one's in-laws. Many teens can't wait to get away from their parents as soon as they turn 18 and start a life of adventure. But we can glean encouragement from our spiritual families as well as our physical families; the more time we spend with them, the more encouraged we can feel. Just imagine how much more Ruth and Naomi were able to encourage each other with their continual presence and kind words.

Naomi acted selflessly, as well. Reread her words in Ruth 1:8, and write them here:

_____

_____

_____

Naomi felt bad that Orpah and Ruth had to be caught up in her problems. Even though Naomi was already starting to feel distressed and discouraged, she did not want others to pity her tragic situation. She did not exclaim, "I'm old, sad and have to move, and that's not fair!" or "Why don't you all come and take care of me? I can't do everything by myself." Even in a time of great

Elizabeth Jimenez

sadness and confusion, she was more concerned about her daughters-in-law than she was about herself. What a great example for the rest of us of how to be encouraging even when times are tough!

➤ Think of a compliment you were given, and share it with the class. What kind of impact did those words have on your day, even your life?

_____

_____

_____

The Example of Elijah

Someone we may not think of as needing much encouragement is the great prophet Elijah. After all, he single-handedly defeated all of the prophets of Baal. Like Naomi, Elijah found himself in an extremely discouraging situation. Unlike Naomi, however, he handled the situation with doubt and self-pity rather than trying to stay positive. Read 1 Kings 19:1-10.

This story teaches us how we should treat those who are feeling down. Ahab and Jezebel were planning to kill Elijah, and like a normal human, Elijah felt scared for his life. Not knowing what to do, he talked to God under a tree. "It is enough!" he cried out. "Now, LORD, take my life, for I am no better than my fathers!" (1 Kings 19:4). Elijah believed he had failed, and he preferred to die at the hands of God than those of men.

Be Persistent

In 1 Kings 19, it was an angel of the Lord who used encouraging words. Write the words of the angel from verse 7:

_____

_____

Elijah ate for 40 days and then retreated to a cave. During that time, God never left his side. Even though God does not directly speak to us anymore, we can always count on Him to be there for us when we're feeling down. Eventually, God asked, "What are you doing here, Elijah?" (1 Kings 19:9). At first, these words may seem bossy instead of encouraging; but God knew what was best for Elijah, and that did not include hiding away and pouting in a cave. When Elijah still did not leave, God repeated the question in verse 13. God did not give up on Elijah; He was persistent.

When we try to encourage others who are feeling down, they may not always respond as quickly as we would like for them to, but our persistence can eventually pay off.

Be Positive

In 1 Kings 19:14, Elijah started to complain and feel sorry for himself.

How did God respond when Elijah complained?

_____

_____

What should our response be when others complain to us?

_____

_____

Sometimes when people feel discouraged, the best way to cheer them up is to help take their minds off the negative emotions they are experiencing; that's exactly what God did with Elijah. In 1 Kings 19:15-17, God gave instructions to Elijah, shifting Elijah's focus from self-pity to positive thinking. As a result, Elijah quickly rose motivated by God's reminder of the "7,000 men who were ready to fight with him." God did not feel angry or disappointed with Elijah; instead, He continued to have faith in his abilities as a great leader, even in his time of greatest distress. Just because of a few simple words, Elijah was able to continue doing great works for the Lord.

Be a Warm Fuzzy

When I was in the sixth grade, my class received brightly colored fuzz balls with glued-on faces called "warm fuzzies." We were to rub the warm fuzzy anytime we experienced low self-esteem or felt down. Do you have a warm fuzzy – someone who can always help you feel better when you're going through a hard time? For Naomi, it was Ruth; for Elijah, it was God. All of us have felt discouraged at times. Hopefully we have someone to cheer us up.

Have you ever experienced a time when you felt like you were the only believer? Where did you find comfort?

_____

_____

_____

Missionaries, in particular, need a lot of encouragement. Before leaving on their trips, they have to decide whether they can truly commit themselves to living in a new place, leaving behind family and friends, and adjusting to a new culture and schedule – not to mention carrying a heavier financial burden. While they are away, they may find themselves wondering: "Am I doing the right thing? Am I the best person for this job? Am I using the most effective approaches in reaching out to others?" They must often depend on friends, family members and fellow church members – their warm fuzzies – to assure them that everything will be okay and that they should not worry about the small things.

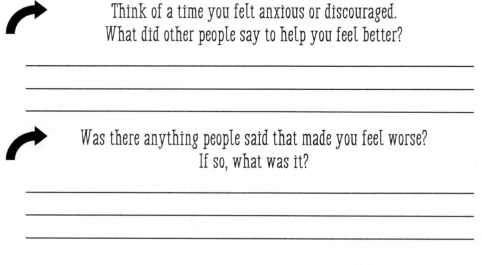

Think of a time you felt anxious or discouraged.
What did other people say to help you feel better?

_____

_____

_____

Was there anything people said that made you feel worse?
If so, what was it?

_____

_____

_____

A Time to Be Consistent

In the end, the best way to encourage others is to always speak in such a way that they will know you love them. Our words should show that we care about and empathize with people and that we sincerely want to see them overcome difficult situations. Remember, a few simple words can go a long way in helping someone feel better.

Practice What You Speak

Group Activity: Compliments Circle

 ## Purpose:

To practice using kind, encouraging words; to develop a stronger bond with other girls in the class.

 ## Instructions:

All of the girls should sit at a table or on the floor in a circle. They should receive a piece of paper and something to write with. At the top of her paper, each girl should write her first and last name and then pass her paper to the girl on her right. Each girl should write something encouraging on the paper about the person whose name is at the top and then sign her own name under her compliment. Keep passing the papers until everyone has written something for each of the other girls and the papers return to their original owners.

Chapter 3

GIVE THANKS

I recently watched a video about an ordinary man going out of his way to help others. For example, he would give his lunch to a homeless boy, help an old lady cross the street in the pouring rain, and pitch in a few dollars a day to a sickly woman collecting money for her daughter to attend school. At the end of the day, he had nothing left except a meager meal in his humble home. But he was happy anyway because he received something much greater: the gratitude of all the people he helped. Now that he had helped them, they were all eager to thank him and do whatever they could to pay it forward. This man serves as a great example of how we should not only help others without expecting something in return but also how we should thank and be considerate of the ones who help us.

"In everything give thanks; for this is the will of God in Christ Jesus for you" (1 Thessalonians 5:18). What does this verse mean to you? To me it means that we should have a constant attitude of thankfulness.

Of the many expressions we utter with our tongues, thankfulness tends to be one of the most difficult. Why do you think we often have a difficult time saying thank you?

_____

_____

_____

Do you have a constant attitude of thankfulness? I don't mean saying a simple "thank you" to the store clerk who bags your items or to the stranger who opens a door for you. I mean going out of your way to genuinely show your appreciation to those who go out of their way for you. Giving thanks is just another way of controlling our tongues so that others will see good fruits in our lives. The more frequently we give thanks, the more frequently we will realize how many wonderful blessings we enjoy and who made those blessings possible in the first place.

> "Oh, give thanks to the Lord, for He is good! For His mercy endures forever" (Psalm 107:1).

Make Time for Thankfulness

Have you ever received a kind note or letter from someone thanking you for something special you did? If so, you know how such a small act can suddenly make your heart feel so big. When we thank others, we cause them to feel loved, appreciated and respected – and who wouldn't want to feel that way? Unfortunately, as with so many things, we don't thank others as much as we should. We tend to focus more on the bad actions people commit than on the good. Instead of letting others know we recognize what they've done, we take their work for granted, quickly forgetting about it before we even say one word to them.

There are several examples in the Bible of people taking for granted Jesus' power to save them. One such example is found in Luke 17:12-19. Of 10 lepers that Jesus healed, only one of them came back to thank Him. The other nine were so busy rejoicing that they did not think to thank the One who made their rejoicing possible. Even though each man was healed, the only one who truly pleased Jesus was the grateful one. Actually, it seems that Jesus was perturbed that only one man came back because He asked: "Were there not ten cleansed? But where are the nine? Were there not any found who returned to give glory to God except this foreigner?" (vv. 17-18).

Sometimes we act selfishly like the nine lepers; we are so focused on ourselves that we don't realize how much other people do to help us. If we don't think about what others have done for us, then we usually won't think about setting aside a special time to thank them. Just think of all the people who have influenced your life to this point. I hope your parents, teachers, friends and youth leaders are at the top of your list. Yet out of all of these people, how many of them have you actually thanked? If the answer is zero, don't feel bad; many of us are guilty of neglecting to show sufficient gratitude. Let the story of the lepers serve to encourage you to be more thankful toward others in the future. From now on, strive to be like the one leper who returned to thank Jesus, rather than the nine who didn't.

How to Be Thankful

Show Your Emotions

The leper who returned instantly to thank Jesus forgot about everything else because he had only one objective: to thank Jesus no matter what. He was a Samaritan (Luke 17:16), and Samaritans generally did not get along well with the Jews. Despite their history, however, nothing could have stopped him from falling down at Jesus' feet and glorifying God. He obviously felt very indebted to Jesus.

When we thank others, they should be able to see that we are excited for what they did just as Jesus could see in the Samaritan man. Any time something wonderful happens, we should be willing to stop everything and thank the person while our emotions are still fresh. Otherwise, if we put off thanking the person, our excitement for what he or she did will diminish, producing less impact. The other nine lepers did not act when they should have. Even if they had decided to go back later and thank Jesus, their gratitude would not have been nearly as powerful as that of the one who came back. Although it is not always possible, we should try to thank others as soon as we can and convey our emotions so they know how much we appreciate what they have done.

Sincere (adjective): having or showing true feelings that are expessesd in an honest way; genuine or real [3]

Be Sincere

The Samaritan man who thanked Jesus was sincere, but too often we thank others out of obligation – not because we really mean what we say. Luke 18:11 says, "The Pharisee stood and prayed thus with himself, 'God, I thank You that I am not like other men – extortioners, unjust, adulterers, or even as this tax collector.' " Not only was the Pharisee arrogant but he was also praying more with his mind than his heart. In order for our prayer to be sincere, it must come from the heart and something we truly feel, not something that we rattle off just because it sounds good.

How was the Pharisee different from the Samaritan leper?

_____

_____

Which of the two men do you think God appreciated more, and why?

_____

_____

Many might argue that the Pharisee was praying to God and trying to do the right thing, so what's the big deal? The problem is he prayed only to show off; he was not being sincere. Unlike the leper, there seemed to be no emotion in his words to show he truly cared about what he was saying; it was as if he were saying "thank you" without even realizing it. Do you ever thank someone blindly, not really thinking about the words you choose and not speaking from your heart? If so, try to be more like the Samaritan man from now on and less like the Pharisee. Most of all, control your tongue by thinking before you speak and showing gratitude mixed with love instead of thank-yous mixed with apathy.

When was a time you should have thanked another person but didn't? Why didn't you?

_____

_____

_____

When was a time you thanked someone insincerely (or a time someone did this to you)? What did you learn from this experience?

_____

_____

_____

As you reflect on the necessity of being more thankful, take a minute to write the names of three people you should thank for making a difference in your life. Then write the words you can use to express your gratitude.

Name: _____

What I can say: _____

Name: _____

What I can say: _____

Name: _____

What I can say: _____

> *"If you want to feel rich, just count all the gifts you have that money can't buy." — Unknown*

Give Thanks to God

Why Should We Thank God?

In addition to thanking our friends and family members, we especially need to give thanks to God. The reasons are endless: He answers our prayers, cares for our families, and guides us through difficult situations. He is our Creator; without Him, we would not even be here.

Name some reasons why we should thank God.

_____

_____

If you are like me, you think more about what you want and need than what God has done for you. But if we don't thank Him, we make ourselves unworthy of receiving such wonderful blessings from Him. Have you ever watched a child quickly open birthday presents one right after another without bothering to thank anyone for them afterward? If we don't thank God for all that He has done for us, we are like that child, so excited about opening the "gift" – whether it be a healed relationship, an answered prayer, or a prized possession – that we don't even remember who it came from, much less thank Him for it.

41

Elizabeth Jimenez

When Should We Thank God?

Psalm 106:1 says: "Praise the LORD! Oh, give thanks to the LORD, for He is good! For His mercy endures forever."

Write Hebrews 13:15 in the space provided.

_____

_____

We don't always need a specific reason to thank God; we could just thank Him in general for the day that He gave us or the beauty of His creation. In fact, a good spiritual goal for your prayer life is to try to remember to thank God for His marvelous acts and immeasurable love every time you pray. At the very least, we should remember to thank Him every time He blesses us (or our families) and every time He answers our prayers.

When you say your next prayer, don't forget to thank God for these answered prayers.

Write down some prayer requests God answered recently – whether for you personally or someone you know. Then go back and circle any you have not yet thanked God for.

_____

_____

_____

_____

A Time to Be Grateful

One of the most positive ways we can use our tongues is to speak words of gratitude to all the people who make a difference in our lives – whether big or small. By doing so, we can touch their lives in the same way they have touched ours. If we don't thank them, these people may believe that we don't appreciate what they have done or that it was all for nothing. The same is true for God. He has done more for us than we deserve, and the least we can do is express sincere gratitude to Him every day. Develop a habit of thanking people more frequently – not just for the petty things and not out of obligation. You may be amazed by the results.

Practice What You Speak
Individual Challenge: Thank You Cards

 Purpose:

To thank someone personally whose work normally goes unnoticed; to experience how rewarding an act of thankfulness can be.

 Instructions:

Think of someone you know who doesn't receive enough recognition for his or her hard work. The person could be a teacher, a preacher, a co-worker, a janitor or even a friend. Now write a note to this person, expressing how much you appreciate what he or she does. Don't forget to mail the note afterward.

Group Activity: Thankfulness Prayer

 Purpose:

To identify everything you have to be thankful for and to thank God for each of these blessings.

 Instructions:

As a group, make a list of everything you are thankful for. Start with the most obvious ideas, like your home and family, and then try to think of more specific blessings, like the talents or opportunities God has provided for you. Challenge yourselves as a group to think of 100 things. Then either have a chain prayer thanking God for those blessings or have a few girls volunteer to lead prayers on behalf of the whole group, mentioning everything from the list.

CONFESS YOUR FAULTS, PART 1

*A*s a teacher, my job consists just as much of teaching kids right from wrong as it does teaching them the curriculum. I constantly have to remind them how to act in the hallway, in the classroom and everywhere we go. One day I noticed a boy was dancing around the desks for no reason than to attract laughs and giggles from his classmates, so I gave him a verbal warning. He immediately went back to his seat, not causing anymore problems. At the end of class, he surprised me by walking up to my desk and saying, "I'm sorry I wasn't doing the right thing. I won't do that anymore." Wow! Talk about being blown away. Most students have the opposite reaction when I reprimand them; they sulk, deny or blame others, never once acknowledging that they made a mistake. This student was only 7 years old, but he knew exactly what to say and how to say it to make amends. Although we are all much older, we sometimes show less maturity than he did because we fail to confess our faults.

Have you asked God to forgive you of a sin lately? I don't just mean saying, "Please forgive me of all the sins I have ever committed. Amen." I mean truly opening up to God with a humble heart and admitting that you need Him to forgive you for the particular sins you have committed. How about to your parents? A close friend or boyfriend? It's not easy for us to admit our mistakes; much less do we want to reveal our deepest, darkest sins. Most of the time we would rather blame someone else than admit we've failed. Why?

Because of our egos. We think only about ourselves and have too much pride to take this step. However, when we do find the courage to confess that we have done something wrong, others will respect us more, and we will prevent hard feelings from turning into hostility.

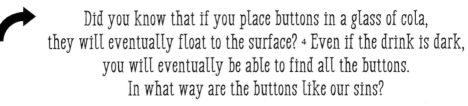

Did you know that if you place buttons in a glass of cola, they will eventually float to the surface? [4] Even if the drink is dark, you will eventually be able to find all the buttons. In what way are the buttons like our sins?

_____

_____

_____

A Sin Versus a Mistake

What is the difference between a sin and a mistake? If you are not sure, ask the people around you what they think, and then write your answer.

_____

_____

_____

All of us make mistakes every day; it may be something as simple as taking the wrong notebook to class or overcooking our supper. A mistake is not usually intentional, and the consequences are not as great. A sin, on the other hand, is normally something we do intentionally, and the consequences are greater. Also, sins are violations of the commands found in God's Word. If the Bible says not to do something and we do it anyway, then we have sinned and need to seek forgiveness. We should admit all of our wrongs, whether they are sins or mistakes – but not necessarily in the same way.

What to Do When We Make a Mistake

After we make a mistake, we should have the courage to admit we have done something wrong. Most likely when we take this step, others will quickly overlook our negligence and forget about what happened. They will also view us as more honorable. If we don't admit our mistakes, however, we may face more criticism later, or our mistakes could even turn into sins – if we lie about them, for instance. Let me give you two examples.

The Relief of Admitting a Mistake

My first job out of college was at an immigration law firm. I was determined to impress my new bosses, but the job proved to be more challenging than I ever realized. About a week after I started, I mischarged a family for their consultation. Unaware that for this particular case I should charge $750, I allowed them to walk into the lawyer's office after paying only $150 – the standard fee. I still remember my boss storming out of her office a few minutes later, looking me in the eye, and exclaiming, "You just lost me $600!" No one had ever talked to me so harshly, and my first instinct was to sprint to the bathroom for a good cry.

Fearful of losing my job, I wrote a long email to my boss explaining that I had made the mistake, that it was completely my fault, and that I was sorry. Now if you think it was easy for me to just take the blame for everything, you're wrong – that's why I had to send an email instead of telling her face to face. Fortunately for me, the message had a lasting effect. My boss was smiling and laughing the next time I saw her, and she never mentioned the incident again.

Think of a time you admitted a mistake to someone. How did that situation turn out? How did you feel afterward?

_____

_____

_____

> "Create in me a clean heart, O God, and renew a steadfast spirit within me" (Psalm 51:10).

The Danger of Covering a Mistake

A few months later, I was working in the same law office, feeling much more confident than I had when I started and even taking on new jobs. One of my new responsibilities was to send visa applications to the national immigration office. Obviously, these were very important documents, and I had to make a copy of everything before sending it as proof of what was sent.

One day I was so busy trying to get my mail-outs done before 5 o'clock that I forgot to make copies of one of them. "Well, that's okay," I thought. "It's too late to do anything about it now anyway; it's already in the mail." About a week later, my boss approached my desk with a scowl on her face.

"Why aren't there copies of the immigration packet in this file?" she demanded.

"I forgot to make copies of it," I admitted sheepishly.

"Why didn't you tell me sooner?"

Good question. At that point, I really didn't know what else to say. All I could do was take the blame and strive to do a better job in the future. But I do know my boss would have been a lot less angry and we may have even found a solution to the problem if I had said something as soon as it happened.

 ### When was a time you did not want to admit a mistake you had made?

_____

_____

 ### Why were you afraid of admitting it?

_____

_____

 ### Did others eventually find out about your mistake? If so, what were the consequences?

_____

_____

Making mistakes is not a sin; all of us do it, and it's nothing to be ashamed of. But when we deliberately try to cover up our mistakes, we turn our mistakes into sins by deceiving others, and we make ourselves look even more foolish. Failing to speak up when we make mistakes is almost the same as denying the action because either way others will be led to believe that we did nothing wrong.

Let's say I accidentally hit the front bumper of a car parked in a parking lot. If no one saw me do it and I drove away without saying anything, is anyone going to know that I was the one who hit the car? Probably not, but I have now committed the sin of trying to hide the truth. If I leave a note with my name and phone number, however, the other driver will have no reason to accuse other motorists falsely, and I can drive away with a clean conscience. In situations like this one, we need to constantly assure ourselves that "Yes, I made a mistake, but yes, I'm big enough to admit that I made this mistake so that I can fix it before it's too late."

Most of the time, we gain very little by trying to hide our mistakes. Sure, maybe no one will find out, but we will not have a clean conscience. When others do find out (which they probably will, at some point), the consequences will be greater because we did not say something as soon as it happened. For example, if we lie to our parents and they find out, we will face a harsher punishment for not being honest in the first place.

The Importance of Confession

Forgiveness Is Necessary for a Clean Heart

Just as we need to be brave enough to admit our mistakes, we also need to ask for forgiveness when we sin. Sometimes it's even more difficult to admit our sins than it is to admit our mistakes. But like the mistakes, these sins will plague us until we find the courage to confess them. Think of your sins as a big, black and nasty stain. Imagine that every time you sin without asking for forgiveness, these black stains cover your heart; the more you sin, the blacker your heart becomes.

On the other hand, if you ask for forgiveness of your sins, God will automatically erase these black stains, leaving your heart clean and strong once again. Write the words of 1 John 1:9-10 in the space provided.

_____

_____

This passage makes it clear that all of us sin and that we all need forgiveness. Which would you rather have: a clean heart free of sin or a black heart full of sin?

Read Isaiah 1:16-18.

What can we compare our dirty clothes to? How do you think your room would smell if you never washed your clothes? How do you think your heart smells to God when you continue to walk in sin?

_____

_____

_____

Confess Now — or on Judgment Day

If we do not confess our sins now, then we will have to confess them on judgment day. God is not going to forget about our sins unless we first ask for His forgiveness. Isaiah 29:15 says: "Look at them! They try to hide things from the Lord. They think he will not understand. They do their evil things in darkness. They tell themselves: 'No one can see us. No one will know who we are' " (ERV). According to this passage, we cannot hide any sins from God. He knows about everything we have done, and He will not be happy with us if we simply try to pretend that we have done nothing wrong.

Matthew 12:36 says, "But I say to you that for every idle word men may speak, they will give account of it in the day of judgment." Likewise, Ecclesiastes 12:14 states, "For God will bring every work into judgment, including every secret thing, whether good or evil." God will not forget our sins until we ask for forgiveness. Which would you prefer: praying for God to forgive you for each sin so that He can erase them one by one or having to explain to God on judgment day why you didn't seek His forgiveness when you had the chance? It's not easy to ask for forgiveness, but it's certainly easier now than it will be on judgment day.

Biblical Examples of Confession

Read the following stories of biblical heroes who had to ask for forgiveness, and answer the questions that follow.

1. Psalm 32:1-5

Who is this passage about? _____

_____

What was his sin? _____

_____

How did he ask for forgiveness? _____

_____

What can we learn from his example? _____

_____

2. Jonah 2

Who is this passage about? _____

What was his sin? _____

_____

How did he ask for forgiveness? _____

_____

What can we learn from his example? _____

_____

3. *Luke 15:11-32*

Who is this passage about? _____

_____

What was his sin? _____

_____

How did he ask for forgiveness? _____

_____

What can we learn from his example? _____

_____

4. *Job 42:1-6*

Who is this passage about? _____

_____

What was his sin? _____

_____

How did he ask for forgiveness? _____

_____

What can we learn from his example? _____

_____

How Can I Know When I Have Sinned?

There are three major ways to know we have sinned and need to ask for forgiveness.

1. Examine Yourself During the Lord's Supper

Read 1 Corinthians 11:27-31, and answer these questions:

What command did Paul give in this passage to all men?

What did he say is the consequence of partaking "in an unworthy manner"?

What happens to those who do not "discern the Lord's body"?

The first step in realizing we have sinned is to examine and judge ourselves. God specifically set aside the time of the Lord's Supper each week for us to think back on our actions and ask ourselves questions such as "Whom did I fail this week, and how?", "Would God be pleased with my actions?", "Did I make good decisions?", and "How can I improve this week on being a better example?" According to 1 Corinthians 11:31, many problems with others could be prevented if we would first judge ourselves. Those who are "weak and sick" (v. 30) are those who have not yet judged themselves. If we partake of the Lord's Supper without examining ourselves, it is like taking for granted Christ's death and the hope of salvation.

2. Read the Bible Regularly

Second Timothy 2:15 says, "Be diligent to present yourself approved to God, a worker who does not need to be ashamed, rightly dividing the word of truth." The more we read the Bible, the more we understand what is right and wrong in God's eyes.

3. Listen to Your Conscience

Whether you have been raised in the church or not, your parents have probably taught you from the time you were a baby what's acceptable behavior and what's not. When we get in trouble for doing something we shouldn't have, it rarely comes as a surprise; we almost always understand that what we did was wrong and expect to face the consequences. James 4:17 says, "Therefore, to him who knows to do good and does not do it, to him it is sin." Most of the time we will know very quickly if something is a sin; if someone offers us a beer, it's not like we have to think for five minutes about it. We know immediately that it's not good, but sometimes we do it anyway. Anytime you feel in your conscience that something is wrong but you do it anyway, you are most likely committing a sin.

> "Judge not, that you be not judged.
> For with what judgment you judge, you will be judged;
> and with the measure you use, it will be measured
> back to you" (Matthew 7:1-2).

A Time for Forgiveness

Every time we make a mistake, we need to have the courage to admit what happened, rather than try to cover it up. Every time we sin, we need to ask forgiveness from God and all those we might have offended. However, just because we make mistakes or fall into temptation, that does not mean we are failures. The Bible makes it clear that everyone is a sinner. The Bible also makes it clear that if we don't ask for forgiveness for the sins we have committed, we continue living in those sins and endanger our chance of living eternally in heaven – even if we have been baptized (Romans 6:1-4, 12). In the next chapter, we will learn about some specific ways we can ask for forgiveness and make our relationship right with God and others.

Practice What You Speak

Group Activity: Sin or Mistake?

 Purpose:

To identify which actions are sins and which are mistakes and to know how to ask correctly for forgiveness in each situation.

 Instructions:

Before class starts, the teacher or class leader should write several activities and situations on index cards – some that are sins, some that are mistakes, and some that are neither. Divide the class into small groups. Provide a set for each group. Have girls from each group take turns reading the cards. In their groups, they will decide if they think it is a sin, mistake or neither. If more than one of the groups has a different answer, have someone from each group explain why the group thinks what it does. (Groups should try to support their answers with biblical passages or examples.)

Chapter #5

CONFESS YOUR FAULTS, PART 2

*E*laine was struggling. A 25-year-old single mother, she had grown up in the church but fallen away five years earlier. Since then, her life had taken a different path: drugs, alcohol, several on and off jobs that led to nowhere, no way to care for her 2-year-old daughter. Then one day, she received a call from an old friend from church. They reignited their friendship, and the friend encouraged Elaine to start attending church again. A few months later, Elaine finally had the courage to pass before the congregation, confess her faults, and seek forgiveness. She instantly received more hugs than any other time in her life. As a result of her confession, the church members helped her become sober, find a stable, better-paying job, and care for her daughter on the days she was not able to. If Elaine had not made the decision to return to church and seek forgiveness, the other members may have never known what a difficult time she was experiencing; she may have lost her daughter, her job, or even her life. Now she thanks God every day for the wonderful way her life turned around, all because of her willingness to confess.

How to Ask for Forgiveness

Once you recognize what sins you are struggling with, you need to ask for forgiveness from whomever you may have offended. There are three major ways to ask for forgiveness.

> *"He who covers his sins will not prosper, but whoever confesses and forsakes them will have mercy"*
> *(Proverbs 28:13).*

1. Pray to God

Normally, if we commit a private sin that does not involve other people, it is only necessary to pray for God to forgive us. For example, if we accidentally say a bad word when no one else is around to hear it, we can pray: "I'm sorry, God, for letting that word slip. Please forgive me and help me not to say this word again." In this case, it is unnecessary to ask forgiveness from others, because we have not offended anyone else.

2. Go to the Person You Offended

On the other hand, if we grow angry with a friend and call her a bad word to her face, we will need to ask forgiveness from God as well as from the friend.

Often the people we offend don't tell us what is wrong. When can you remember someone actually saying "I'm so disappointed in you" or "I can never think of you the same way again"? But just because others don't tell us they are offended doesn't mean they have accepted what we did.

So how can you know when you have offended someone? Most of the time, it will be obvious; that person won't want to talk to you as much, or he or she might scowl at you instead of smile. Sometimes we offend others without realizing it or without meaning to do anything wrong. In this case, we can pray for God to help us see our faults. We can also ask Him to help us not to offend others and to repair relationships with any people we might have already offended.

If all else fails, use your common sense. Almost any time you do something you know you're not supposed to do or something that doesn't feel right, chances are someone won't like it – whether it is your friends, your boyfriend, your parents, etc. Remember that even when no one else finds out about our sins, God always knows. As our heavenly Father, He will feel just as disappointed in us as our earthly parents.

3. Go Before Your Church Family

When we do something that might offend some or several members of the church, it is necessary to also respond to the Lord's invitation and ask for forgiveness in front of the congregation. Examples of acts for which we need to ask for the church's forgiveness include sexual sins, stealing, cheating and sometimes even lying and gossiping (which we will talk more about in part 2 of this book).

Although it's not always necessary to ask forgiveness from the whole church family, it can help us feel better about any of the sins we commit. For example, the girl who called her friend a bad name doesn't necessarily have to confess to the whole church what she did, but she might feel better asking the church to forgive her for not being the kind of Christian example she needed to be. She could also ask her church family to help her make better decisions in the future.

Like throwing off your heavy backpack as soon as you get home from school, asking the church for strength and forgiveness relieves you of a cumbersome burden.

Write James 5:16 in the space provided:

_____

_____

If our Christian brothers and sisters truly care about us and have the love of Christ, then they will shower us with support and prayers when we confess our sins, rather than with criticism and complaints.

Confession is also pleasing to God. Luke 15:7 states, "I say to you that likewise there will be more joy in heaven over one sinner who repents than over ninety-nine just persons who need no repentance." Isn't it comforting to know that our Christian brothers and sisters will wrap us in love and that God will rejoice just because we confessed our sin? And remember that God does not put a size on sin; no matter what the sin is, whether we think it's serious or not, we need to ask for forgiveness.

Try to think of some other times when we might need to ask for forgiveness, and write them in the space provided.

Private sins we only need to ask God to forgive us of:_____

_____

Sins we need to ask friends or family members to forgive us of: _____

_____

Sins we need to ask the whole church to forgive us of: _____

_____

Other Points to Consider

Ask With Sincerity

It is very important that when we ask for forgiveness, we do so sincerely. Otherwise, we have not fully acknowledged the sinfulness of the act, and we will continue living with this sin. Sometimes we may have to ask for forgiveness several times before the person can fully forget about what happened and treat us the same way. When we have a sincere heart, though, the other person is more likely to forgive us the first time we ask. Can you remember a time when someone apologized with his or her head down and eyes darting in different directions? Most likely this person was not sincere, and the person being apologized to felt no different afterward. If you have to apologize to someone, keep your head up, look the person in the eyes, and say it like you mean it.

Read Genesis 3:13.
Who did Eve blame for her sin? Have you ever used the excuse "the devil made me do it" to explain away your sin?

_____

_____

_____

_____

Remember that even though S.atan may tempt you, he cannot make you do anything. You always have a choice and a way of escape (1 Corinthians 10:13).

Avoid Blaming and Lying

In my first year teaching, I asked a student to give me his cellphone because he was using it during class. Later I found out he intentionally deceived me by giving me another girl's cellphone, and she didn't know anything about it. The next day I held the two after class and told him to explain to the girl what he had done. "Well, don't worry about it," he said, "because thanks to Mrs. Jimenez my mom took my phone away. I don't have a phone now because of her." Never once did he own up to what he did or say, "I'm sorry that I took your cellphone."

Adam and Eve also chose to blame others instead of confessing their sins to God. Read Genesis 3:1-19, and answer the questions that follow.

1. Whom did Adam blame for eating the fruit of the tree of the knowledge of good and evil?

2. Whom did Eve blame for eating the fruit?

Of course God knew exactly when, why and how Adam and Eve committed their sins. Yet it still pained Him to hear them try to cover up what they had done rather than just admitting it.

1. What was Adam's punishment for his sin?

2. What was Eve's punishment?

3. Do you think God would have still punished Adam and Eve if they had admitted their failure instead of trying to hide it? Why, or why not?

When you get in trouble for something, don't cause others to look bad because you're too proud to tell the truth. The faster you tell what happened, the faster the ordeal will be over, and the faster others will forget about it – and possibly even thank you for the truthful explanation. The consequences will almost always be less severe when we admit our wrongs rather than trying to hide them.

It is just as important that we don't allow our lack of courage to ignite lies. Sarah lied that she didn't laugh when she heard she would have a baby in her old age, and the Lord caught her in the act (Genesis 18:15). It did not help Sarah to deny what she did; it only made the situation more awkward for her.

Write an example of a time you lied to avoid confessing something you did wrong.

_____

_____

_____

What happened as a result of the lie?

_____

_____

_____

A good apology has three parts:
1. "I'm sorry."
2. "It's my fault."
3. "What can I do to make it right?"

What Should I Say?

Asking for forgiveness doesn't just mean that you say to someone, "Will you forgive me?" As we have already seen, simply saying "I'm sorry" is one way. You could also talk privately to the people who seem offended with you and ask them directly: "What did I do to bother you? Whatever it is, I didn't mean to, and I'm sorry. I won't let it happen again."

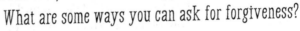 What are some ways you can ask for forgiveness?

_____

_____

A Time for Self-Reflection

Read through the following prompts and questions about forgiveness. Answer them in the space provided.

A sin I need to be forgiven of:

What I will do to ask for forgiveness of this sin:

When was a time someone had to apologize to you or ask for your forgiveness?

Did the person seem sincere? Why, or why not?

Those who can admit their mistakes and sins will find the support of those who care about them. They will be more respected, have better relationships, and have a purer heart. They will also have the assurance of knowing they have done what God wants them to do. Those who consistently insist that they've done nothing wrong or blame others, on the other hand, have not fully come to understand God's desire for them. They are selfish, egotistical and self-centered. If you have recognized sins in your life, don't be one of those people who refuses to believe that anything is wrong or who tries to cover up the bad behavior, only making the situation worse and allowing the sin to become a stumbling block to herself or to others. Be someone who can admit your faults and learn from them.

Practice What You Speak
Individual Challenge: Improvement List

 Purpose:

To recognize the areas in which you can improve as a Christian and to seek forgiveness for each of the sins you have committed.

 Instructions:

As you examine yourself during the Lord's Supper each week, identify three sins you have committed in the past week. If you have not sinned, identify three areas in which you need to improve. It could be something small and personal, mistakes you have made, sins you committed just one time, or sins you struggle with consistently. After church, write what the three sins/areas for improvement are, and write one goal of what you can do to improve each one. Make sure that if it is a sin, you note whom you need to ask to forgive you. Try to do this part as soon as possible, before you forget.

Check the paper periodically during the week to make sure you're striving to reach your goals. If it is a sin or mistake you committed just one time, you will hopefully be able to complete your goal before the following Sunday. Some consistent sins or areas of improvement may take longer for you to reach the goal than just one week, but you can continue to include them in the three items if you believe you have not yet reached the goal. Continue making a new list (or adding to the same one) each week until you develop the habit of recognizing your sins and receiving forgiveness for each one. Below is an example.

Week of _____

Sins/Areas for Improvement	Goals
1. Didn't pray much.	Pray at least once every day.
2. Talked badly about my friend.	Talk to her; tell her I didn't mean to.
3. Disobeyed my mom.	Tell her I'm sorry, and I learned my lesson.

Chapter #6

SPREAD THE GOOD NEWS

I have been on a lot of mission trips and seen a lot of great acts, but there is one incident that particularly stands out. It was a Wednesday, another scorching day in El Salvador and the point in the week when people start to feel discouraged. I had been working with kids inside the church building all day, but I stepped outside just long enough to wash my hands. Across the street, I noticed a woman barely in her 30s sitting with two kids. I explained to the woman that we were having children's classes and invited them to come, but she was talking on the phone at the time and waved her hands like she couldn't be disturbed. A few minutes later, another girl from our group saw that the lady was still talking on the phone and began playing peek-a-boo with the two children. Little by little the children moved closer to the class, until finally they decided to join us, and the mother had no choice but to sit in the back and watch. Another lady from our group invited her to come have a Bible study. She reluctantly agreed.

After studying and learning the truth, she decided to get baptized. Tears streamed down her face after her baptism as she exclaimed how happy she was. I never thought that one invitation, along with several other servants helping along the way, would end in a precious soul being added to the church. If I hadn't gone to wash my hands in just that exact moment, or if the other girl hadn't had the foresight to play with the children, or if the other lady hadn't had the courage to study the Bible with her, this struggling mother may have never come to know God and His love for her.

Elizabeth Jimenez

If you have ever participated in a mission trip, you understand how reward-ing it feels to share the gospel with others. Yet for some reason, when we return from the mission trip and back to the real world, we often don't have the same zeal to continue saying great things about our Savior. We can travel around the world to talk about the Bible through a translator to people we have never seen before, but we can't say one word to the people we come in contact with every day.

Why do you think we have a hard time sharing the gospel on a daily basis?

_____

_____

Why do you think it is important for us to tell others about Jesus?

_____

_____

> { *"And He said to them, 'Go into all the world and preach the gospel to every creature. He who believes and is baptized will be saved; but he who does not believe will be condemned'"* (Mark 16:15-16). }

Why Should We Preach the Gospel?

It Is a Command

One reason spreading the good news is so important is because the Great Commission is a command. Read Matthew 28:19-20, and write the Great Commission in the space provided:

_____

_____

_____

Jesus spoke these words, and they are just as much a commandment as "you shall not murder" (Exodus 20:13) or "you shall not steal" (v. 15). Yet we tend to think of the Great Commission as less important – something we should do if we can, but not something we have to do.

So many people in other parts of the world are living in sin and don't know Jesus. If we don't follow this commandment, these people may die without ever being offered the hope of eternal life, and we will be partly responsible. What a shame.

Curious about how many people in our country claim to be Christians, I read *Good News and Bad News: A Realistic Assessment of Churches of Christ in the United States 2008*, by Flavil Yeakley. Although there has been some growth in the churches of Christ, there is still much more work to do be done – proving that each and every one of us needs to do everything possible to reach the lost and falling away souls that are all around us. Let's take a look at some of the most eye-opening statistics:

• Of the 13,000 congregations of churches of Christ in the U.S., about half (45 percent) have fewer than 50 members. Only 30 percent of congregations have more than 100 members.

• A study conducted by the Association of Statisticians of American Religious Bodies ranked churches of Christ as number 12 out of 14 in the list of top Christian groups, with the Catholic religion being number one.

• The same study found that there are at least 250 religious groups in our country claiming to be "Christian."

• More than half of Americans who identify themselves as church of Christ live in only five states: Texas, Tennessee, Alabama, Arkansas and Oklahoma.

• From 1980 to 2006, churches of Christ in the United States grew by only 2.1 percent in members and 1.9 percent in new congregations.

• Only 30 percent of the 7 billion people living throughout the world claim to be Christian.

These statistics do not lie. Since the church of Christ is still outnumbered by many religious groups, we have a great responsibility to share the gospel with others. The need becomes even greater in other parts of the world where the majority of people do not even call themselves Christian. According to Yeakley, only half of all U.S. citizens identify themselves as members of any

> **Responsibility (noun):**
> a duty or task that you
> are required or expected to do;
> something that you should
> do because it is morally right,
> legally required, etc. [5]

Christian group – and many of them do not attend church regularly. Even those of us who live in an area where the church of Christ is more prominent face the challenge of teaching those who either don't attend church at all or are part of other religious groups.[6]

One of the many positive ways we can use our mouths is to speak a good word for Jesus. It might not cause anyone to come to church with us or be baptized or request a Bible study, but at least the people we talk to will know what we believe. Also, we will have the satisfaction of knowing that we shared the good news, rather than trying to hide it.

It Is Our Responsibility

Remember that according to the Great Commission, we have a responsibility – not a choice – to share the gospel with every creature. Paul understood better than most that it was urgent to preach the gospel and that there would be consequences if he did not fulfill this duty. In 1 Corinthians 9:16, he said, "For if I preach the gospel, I have nothing to boast of, for necessity is laid upon me; yes, woe is me if I do not preach the gospel!" He considered preaching the gospel a necessity, and he was actually worried about what would happen to him if he did not preach the gospel rather than worrying about what would happen to him if he did preach. I wonder how many more preachers and teachers there would be nowadays if more of us had this attitude.

Everyone deserves to hear the gospel, and God wants us to share it with as many people as possible. It doesn't matter what they look like, where they're from, what their current ideas are, or where they live – we still need to reach out to them. Paul described how he felt about preaching to the Gentiles in Ephesians 3:8-9:

> To me, who am less than the least of all the saints, this grace was given, that I should preach among the Gentiles the unsearchable riches of Christ, and to make all see what is the fellowship of the mystery, which from the beginning of the ages has been hidden in God who created all things through Jesus Christ.

Originally, the apostles were hesitant to preach to the Gentiles, but once they did, the church grew and grew. If each of us does her part to share the good news and tell others about Jesus, then the church can grow all over the world.

God is counting on each one of us to help Him carry out His work here on the earth. Luke 4:43 says, "But He said to them, 'I must preach the kingdom of God to the other cities also, because for this purpose I have been sent.' " In this passage, Jesus was explaining to the multitude that followed Him why He could not stay with them longer. We know that Jesus stayed very busy traveling from place to place to tell about His kingdom, and that was one reason God sent Him to live on the earth. Now that Jesus has ascended to heaven, we have the great responsibility of continuing His work.

Jesus and the apostles were able to perform miracles to help the people believe, but now the only way to teach about Jesus is by the Bible – and our mouths. Almost everyone has access to a Bible, but what use is it to them if they don't understand the majority of passages in it because no one ever took the time to sit down and explain it to them? If we don't fulfill God's work of teaching others, the world will be deceived by false prophets – all because we did not have the courage to speak the truth.

Even though women cannot be preachers in the traditional sense, how can they still spread the gospel? How can you spread the gospel?

_____

_____

_____

_____

How Can We Teach Others?

Take Advantage of Every Opportunity

We should take advantage of every opportunity to tell others about the gospel. Just because we cannot go on a mission trip to another country does not mean we cannot evangelize. God provides us opportunities every day through the people all around us, and He expects us to seize those opportunities. That does not mean we have to preach a sermon to all of our friends. If someone is going through a hard time, we could simply quote a verse from the Bible that pertains to his or her situation. If a group of friends is wondering what will happen to us when we die, we can describe what heaven will be like and briefly explain how we can achieve a home in heaven.

What are some other ways we can tell others about the gospel?

What are some specific examples of situations we should take advantage of to tell others about the gospel?

Acts 8:4 says, "Therefore those who were scattered went everywhere preaching the word." At that time, Saul had been persecuting the church, and the early Christians were scattered as a result. But they did not let these problems deter them from continuing to preach and spread the gospel. Instead, they viewed them as opportunities to preach even more.

We can often reach out to others during times of crisis. Several years ago, when Hurricane Katrina ravaged Louisiana and Mississippi, some Christians started making trips to these areas to help rebuild houses. In their many trips, they were able to develop a relationship with the people they were helping and tell them about Jesus. Eventually, the victims became more and more curious about the gospel, and some decided to be baptized. Now new churches exist in Louisiana and Mississippi – all because of the desire to turn a catastrophe into an opportunity to spread the Word.

> "Never forget the power of one."
> — Unknown

Do Your Part to Make a Difference

Sometimes we believe we can only do so much to grow God's kingdom, so why bother? But if all of us had the attitude that one person can't accomplish anything, the church would never grow. One person can make a tremendous difference. Even though a mission trip is a team effort, it takes just one person to leave materials on someone's door or invite someone to church. Those who participate in foreign mission trips and don't speak the local language must depend on a translator to communicate; the translator is just one person providing the vital connection between the hearers and the sowers. Think of all the people you know who have single-handedly held

Bible studies with someone, invited that person to church, and then had the privilege of baptizing him or her. Just because you are young and on your own doesn't mean you can't save souls too. We should want to save souls and make every effort to do so.

How is a Christian spreading the gospel like a domino?

_____

_____

Have Courage, Not Fear

The apostles serve as excellent examples of speaking excitedly about Jesus without fear. In Acts, the apostles faced great persecution for preaching about Jesus. In chapter 5, they had already been thrown in prison by the high priest; however, that did not stop them from continuing to preach the good news when they were freed. Acts 5:29-30 says: "But Peter and the other apostles answered and said: 'We ought to obey God rather than men. The God of our fathers raised up Jesus whom you murdered by hanging on a tree.' " What shameless courage these men had. Verse 40 continues, "And when they had called for the apostles and beaten them, they commanded that they should not speak in the name of Jesus, and let them go."

If you knew you would be thrown into prison for preaching the gospel, what would you do? Could you still be as zealous as the apostles were? Most of us have never been beaten up, much less have we been beaten up for talking about Jesus. If we had been in the predicament of the apostles, we might have thought: "I need to protect myself, so it's okay if I stop talking about Jesus. God will understand." But read Acts 5:41.

How did the apostles react?

_____

Again, the apostles showed no remorse for what was happening to them. They did not make excuses, nor did they try to escape from or avoid their persecutors. Instead, they "departed from the presence of the council, rejoicing that they were counted worthy to suffer shame for His name" (Acts 5:41). They rejoiced because they suffered for speaking about Jesus. I hope all of us can experience happiness when we tell others about Jesus as well.

What can we learn from the apostles' example in Acts 5?

Did the apostles continue to speak the good news about Jesus even after the council warned them not to? (If you are not sure, scan through the next chapters in Acts.)

List some ways people "suffer" today for talking about Jesus. Have you experienced any of these?

_____

_____

_____

Be Proud, Not Ashamed

Read Matthew 26:69-75, and answer these questions:

1. What were some of the specific words Peter used when he denied Jesus?

2. How do you think Jesus felt when Peter denied Him?

3. What did Peter do when he realized he had denied Jesus?

4. What are some ways we deny Jesus?

Peter was one of Jesus' best friends, so just imagine how Jesus must have felt when Peter said "I do not know the Man" (Matthew 26:72). When we have an opportunity to tell others about Jesus but don't say anything, it is as if we are denying Him. After all, how will others ever know how we feel about Jesus, His church and God's Word if we don't ever tell them? Paul wrote in Romans 1:16, "For I am not ashamed of the gospel of Christ, for it is the power of God to salvation for everyone who believes, for the Jew first and also for the Greek." Can you honestly say you are not ashamed of the gospel? If so, you should be able to talk about religious topics as openly as you can talk about clothes and accessories, and it doesn't bother you one bit when others ask you questions about your faith. If this is not you, then seek God's help to have more courage or the wisdom to choose just the right words.

When I was younger, sporting events frequently occurred on Wednesday nights. My parents did not allow me to miss church to participate in the games, but I never liked approaching my coaches and telling them this. I was ashamed of the gospel, and I was denying Jesus. God knows what we're thinking, so He will know very quickly if we are sincerely trying to spread His Word or secretly trying to keep it under wraps. And Jesus can still feel the same pain and disappointment with us that He felt with His disciples.

When was a time you felt ashamed of the gospel or denied Jesus?

_____

_____

How did you feel about the situation afterward?

_____

_____

Those of you who are already baptized, remember how excited you felt when you first came out of the water? The past was behind you; you were a new creature, and you were on fire for Jesus. We should have that same excitement every day. Instead of feeling ashamed of the gospel or denying Jesus, we should share with others how wonderful we felt about being baptized and what a blessing it is to be a Christian. Even if you are not yet a baptized Christian, you can still share why you go to church or what Jesus means to you.

A Time to Evangelize

Spreading the gospel means a lot more than giving someone a new Bible or having a religious discussion. Here are some examples of other ways to evangelize:

- Invite others to church.

- Give them an encouraging verse to read, or read it to them yourself.

- Share a Bible story with others that applies to their current situation.

- Tell people you're praying for them.

- Offer assistance in times of need.

Elizabeth Jimenez

Think of three people in your life who need to understand the power of the gospel. Write their names and what you can do for each one.

1._____

2._____

3._____

Jesus commanded us to "preach the gospel to every creature" (Mark 16:15). He is depending on us to tell others about Him. If we don't, we are denying Him, and He will feel only heartache and disappointment as a result. On the other hand, when we try to speak to others, we could help bring a soul closer to salvation. Jesus will recognize our efforts, and we will feel better about ourselves. Christ died for us, so there is no reason for us to be ashamed of Him. Instead, we owe it to Him to tell as many people as possible what He has done for us and what He can do for them. The next time you have an opportunity to speak a good word for Jesus, try to show more passion and excitement for your Savior. You never know what the effect of your words may be, but most likely it will only be good.

Practice What You Speak
Individual Challenge: Suffering Souls

 ## Purpose:

To seek out and make an impact on those who need to hear the gospel the most.

 ## Instructions:

Often, those who are suffering are the ones who need to learn about Jesus the most. Identify three people you don't know very well who seem to be suffering. It could be someone sitting by herself in the school cafeteria, the cashier at the store who just looks sad, or the girl on the volleyball team whose parents are always yelling at her. Approach these people confidently, and choose one of the ways mentioned in the chapter to reach out to them and bring them closer to knowing Jesus. You may be amazed at how receptive they are and just how much they are willing to do to change their lives for the better – even if it means going to church with a complete stranger.

Group Activity: Class Flier Project

 ## Purpose:

To design a flier for young people that makes them more interested in coming to church or learning about Jesus.

 ## Instructions:

Work together to design a flier about the church, the youth group, or an upcoming event. Make it especially relevant to young people, and design it in such a way that it will quickly get their attention. Be sure to include the church's address, phone number and website. Use the next week to put the finishing touches on the flier. The teacher or class leader should then make copies and pass them out for each girl to give some to her friends. Each girl should be sure to invite her friends personally, not just hand them the flier.

The teacher or class leader could also put the girls' evangelizing skills to practice by scheduling a day for the class to talk to other young people at a local hang-out spot, such as the skate park or the mall, and pass out fliers to those they meet.

PART 2

Salty, Bitter
WORDS

SAY NO TO GOSSIP, PART 1

*S*helley had a burning secret. Not wanting to keep it to herself any longer, she finally decided to share it with her best friend Kristen, pleading with her not to tell anyone else. But Kristen accidentally let the secret slip while she was talking to Jennifer ... who then told Will ... who then told Gabi ... who then told everyone on the soccer team. By the end of the day, more than half of the school had learned what was supposed to be confidential information between two friends.

Have you ever been the victim of gossip? You know what I'm talking about – when you say something to a friend, then she tells her friend, then another friend, and on and on until what you told the first friend (that she promised never to tell anyone) has become a twisted, contorted mess of words nothing like the original sentence. How did it make you feel to know that others were talking badly about you?

What Is Gossip?

Before we continue, let's make sure we understand what gossip really is. Sure, you know what it means, but do you realize when you're doing it? Do you understand which gossip is bad and which is good (if any)? Do you notice the negative effects it causes afterward? Take a minute to answer the questions on the next page.

1. In your own words, what is gossip?

2. Do you struggle with gossip? If so, what do you gossip about the most?

3. Have you ever gossiped about someone, and then that person found out about it? If so, what were the consequences?

4. Can you think of any instances when gossip is good? If so, what?

Gossip can be anytime we talk about someone when he or she doesn't know about it and would not approve of what we are saying. Rumors result from gossip and are usually not true, but someone can tell the truth and still be gossiping. Sometimes we may even have good intentions in talking about the person. For example, Mary might tell Cindy, "Did you hear that Lauren is going to have a baby?" Mary is speaking the truth; it's good news, and she's excited about it. But maybe Lauren didn't want Mary to tell Cindy that she's going to have a baby; maybe Lauren was waiting to tell Cindy herself, and now she can't. Unless you have the person's full approval, it's probably best not to share any personal details about her with others – whether good or bad.

Have you ever caught someone gossiping about you? How did you feel? What did you learn from the experience?

_____

_____

_____

Why Should We Avoid Gossip?

There are many reasons we should avoid gossip, all of which are equally important. If you have ever discovered people gossiping about you, you probably understand why we should do everything possible to prevent it from spreading. There are seven key reasons that we will focus on.

1. It Causes Others to Mistrust Us

If you start to talk about other people behind their backs, the people around you will notice. They will notice that you are not very respectful toward others, and they will notice that you obviously have nothing better to do with your time. Then they might start thinking, "Does she talk about me when I'm not around?" Or maybe they won't want to tell you anything because they're afraid you will tell others. Have you ever decided not to spend as much time around someone because you noticed he or she was always talking about other people? If so, you made a good decision. Even those who are closest to us cannot be expected to trust us if we constantly use our tongues to gossip rather than edify.

2. It Destroys Friendships

When I was 5 years old, I was stepping off the school bus one day when my friend Megan whispered in my ear which boy she had a crush on. She asked me not to tell anyone, but the first thing I did was run and shout loud enough for the whole neighborhood to hear: "Megan likes John! Megan likes John!" Granted, 5-year-olds know little about relationships. But I knew just from the look on Megan's face that she was mad and disappointed with me. To this day, I painfully remember breaking a promise to a friend – all for no good reason.

If we treat our friends' secrets like nothing more than candy being thrown at a parade, there's a good chance we will lose our friends and be labeled as mean and immature. Naturally, Megan never wanted to share another secret with me after that day. Who can blame her?

Proverbs 16:28 says, "A perverse man sows strife, and a whisperer separates the best of friends." Are you a whisperer? Do you like to gather around your friends and share juicy tidbits about others and then quickly change the topic when someone walks in the room? Rather than being the kind of friend who starts wildfires with her words, we should be the kind who tries to put out the fires.

> "There would be far fewer problems in life if we just started talking to each other instead of about each other."
> — Unknown

3. It Causes Others to Have a Negative Perception of Us

Let's say you are with a group of friends talking about your plans for the weekend when one of you spots a classmate walking by. Without thinking, you say: "Hey, look at her. I heard that her boyfriend wants to break up with her because he likes another girl." Now let's say that at the same time you say this, an elder from your church walks by and hears everything. Would he be ashamed to hear you speak this way? Or would he think this kind of behavior is normal for you and think nothing of it? Whatever the answer, he would certainly not walk away thinking that you're a model Christian, which is what we all should strive to be every day.

Now imagine the person you are talking about hears what you said. This girl will most certainly find you rude and inconsiderate – not thoughtful, loving or encouraging. Even when we think we are talking in privacy, there is always a chance that others will find out. Therefore, we need to be careful not to say anything that could blow up in our faces afterward. In chapter 2, we talked about how important it is to reach out to others. How will we ever reach these people if they see us talking bad about them rather than befriending them and surrounding them with love?

4. It Hurts Our Chances of Finding Good Friends

If we want to have good friends, we need to first be a good friend. If we want to be good Christians, we need to choose friends who are striving to be pure and acceptable also. People will have a hard time trusting us or will have a bad impression of us if they notice we are constantly talking about others. Also, they may get bored hearing the same conversations over and over again. If you want to have good friends, try choosing only neutral topics to talk about that will not offend anyone, and avoid sticking your nose in other people's business.

{
"Lord, who may abide in Your tabernacle? Who may dwell in Your holy hill? He who walks uprightly, and works righteousness, and speaks the truth in his heart; he who does not backbite with his tongue, nor does evil to his neighbor, nor does he take up a reproach against his friend" (Psalm 15:1-3).
}

5. It Is Foolish

In the majority of cases, what we say when we gossip is not necessary and could easily be substituted with something more respectful. Instead of talking about someone being a rich, spoiled brat, you could talk about why parents (in general) give their kids so many belongings they don't deserve or need. Instead of talking others, talk about someone you would like to know better and how to do that.

Think of a time you gossiped about someone. What is something else you could have said that would have been better?

There is no purpose in gossiping about others except to be heard. Maybe we do it to fit in, but as we saw earlier, gossip can actually make it harder to keep good friends.

Copy the verses in the space provided.

Proverbs 10:31:_____

Ecclesiastes 10:12:_____

Because the opposite of wisdom is foolishness, either you are bringing forth wisdom, or you are bringing forth foolishness. If you talk about others unnecessarily, you are speaking foolishness. We can see from these verses that God does not approve of foolish, perverse speaking and that gossipers will have their punishment.

6. It Distorts the Truth

James 3:5 says: "Even so the tongue is a little member and boasts great things. See how great a forest a little fire kindles!" When we gossip, our words are like fire. Every time we talk foolishly about another person, we start a new fire. Then, the people we tell spread the fire. Think of each person who spreads our words as a tree and the large group of people who hear the words – such as the whole school – as the forest. The number of people burned by the fire rapidly multiplies, and the quality of the words (if there was any to begin with) is quickly diminished while the fire grows larger and larger. We may start out saying just three words, but after several people hear, the words evolve into a long, drawn-out story. Just imagine how false the story can be after it travels through so many mouths with so many personal touches and versions and characters added along the way.

Not only does what we say when we gossip rapidly turn into lies, but it often causes us to judge others unfairly – sometimes without actually knowing the people involved. Teachers who spend a lot of time in the teachers' lounge are known to talk badly about students. In fact, sometimes they talk negatively about students so much that other teachers develop a misguided opinion of students they don't even know. For example, a teacher might think: "There's Johnny. He's the one that Mrs. Bryant says is always so rude." Before the teacher even meets the student, she is already thinking bad thoughts about him. These judgments based on gossip will make it harder for the teacher to help the student and give him a fair chance to succeed. Similarly, mean comments we hear about our classmates may cause us to think unfair thoughts and to make little or no effort to show them kindness.

We need to make sure we're not talking about others in a way that will cause anyone to have a negative perception of them. We also need to remember that not all gossip we hear about others is true.

7. It Cannot Be Kept Secret

Even if they don't find out that we were gossiping about them, God always knows. Hebrews 4:13 states, "And there is no creature hidden from His sight, but all things are naked and open to the eyes of Him to whom we must give account." Likewise, in Mark 4:22, we read that "there is nothing hidden which will not be revealed, nor has anything been kept secret but that it should come to light."

What do these verses mean to you?

_____

_____

To me they mean that no sin is ever truly secret including gossip. God is aware of all of our words and actions. When we gossip about others, we offend our heavenly Father. Most of the time, the people we were gossiping about will somehow find out our "secret" and become offended, as well. Can you think of a time that someone never discovered others were gossiping about her? I can't.

A few years ago, on a mission trip in Honduras, some girls were sitting in a hotel room talking. The conversation started out normally, but one thing led to another, and before long, they were talking badly about another girl from the group. Even the kindest girls found themselves joining in the conversation and agreeing with the others. That's how gossip is; it starts out subtly but pulls you in gradually until, eventually, you don't even realize what you're saying or why – like the currents of the ocean's waves that start out calm and then lure you into a riptide without warning. Their talk seemed innocent until the next day when the girl they were talking about approached them in tears demanding to know why they were talking about her. Naturally, her so-called friends were speechless and humiliated.

Think about some of the times you have talked badly about someone, whether intentionally or not. Could you have repeated the same words to the person's face? Probably not. Unless you want other people to know what you're saying about them, keep your comments to yourself. Otherwise, if the person does find out, prepare yourself for the confrontation that will follow.

A Time to Be Positive

When we use our tongues to talk badly about others, we accomplish nothing. Our tongues should be a fountain of positive words to help and encourage, rather than betray and bring down. Gossiping almost always brings negative consequences – not only for the person talking, but also for the person being talked about. If you have a hard time controlling your tongue when others are gossiping or you like to talk a lot and the next thing you know you're talking about someone without meaning to, then don't worry; you're not alone. But continue reading to find out what you can do to control your tongue in these situations and avoid gossiping.

Practice What You Speak

Individual Challenge: Gossip Substitutes

 Purpose:

To recognize what we gossip about the most and to practice changing the negative things we say into something positive.

 Instructions:

Most of the time when we gossip, we talk badly about another person. For the activity below, think of people you have a tendency to gossip about. In the first column, write what you would normally say about that person or group of people, and in the second column, write what you could say so that it is no longer gossip. The first row has been done for you as an example.

Now challenge yourself to remember the positives you wrote about this person or group of people so that the next time you are tempted to gossip, you keep the negatives to yourself and say the positives instead.

What I Normally Say	What I Could Say Instead
She is selfish and arrogant.	*She wears really nice clothes.*

Words, Meaningless Words

by Elizabeth Jimenez

Words
Meaningless words
Passing along
Like candy
Everyone happy to receive them
Even when they're not sweet.

Rumors
Cruel rumors
Falling on foolish ears
Sometimes true, sometimes not
Torturing the victim
For weeks to come.

Gossip
Unnecessary gossip
Inflicting pain, disappointment, rage
A senseless way to pass the time
Spreading like wildfire
If no one speaks out.

Chapter #8

SAY NO TO GOSSIP, PART 2

*L*et's refresh our memories with what we learned about gossip in the previous chapter.

What are at least two specific reasons we should not gossip?

Of the seven reasons we should not gossip mentioned in chapter 7, which do you think is most important, and why?

Read 1 Timothy 5:13-14. What did Paul say about the young widows in this verse?

What advice did he give them regarding gossip in verse 14?

Paul was disappointed that the widows spent so much of their time gossiping and encouraged them not to give place to the devil. We read of a similar warning in Proverbs 20:19: "He who goes about as a talebearer reveals secrets; therefore do not associate with one who flatters with his lips." From these scriptures, we can clearly understand the importance of avoiding gossip (and gossipers).

Elizabeth Jimenez

How Can We Avoid Gossip?

Now that you understand what gossiping is and why you should avoid it, we will examine four methods for *how* you can avoid it.

> What kind of emergency situations might require
> you to share information you were asked not to tell?
> What should you do in such a situation?

_____

_____

_____

_____

_____

1. Remain Silent

It's always better to maintain silence than to say something we will regret. When we hear something about another person that we don't know for sure is true, we should remain silent. When a friend tells us a secret and we promise not to tell anyone, we should remain silent. Even if our friend doesn't specifically tell us "don't tell anyone," we should use common sense and know when the information is appropriate to repeat and when it's not. In most instances, there's no need to repeat the words unless in an emergency.

> Write 1 Peter 3:4 in the space provided:

_____

_____

_____

_____

Those who are constantly gossiping and spreading rumors certainly do not have the gentle and quiet spirit described in this verse. Christian girls, on the other hand, can exemplify this spirit by minding their own business and refraining from talking badly about others.

2. Defend the Person

When you hear others talking badly about someone, don't be afraid to stand up for the person. Wouldn't you want others to do the same for you? For example, you might hear someone say, "George cries like a baby every time he gets a bad grade." You could say: "At least he's worried about his education. That's better than some people who don't come to class or even try." If you hear something that sounds off the wall,

> *Before you speak, think:*
> *T – Is it true?*
> *H – Is it helpful?*
> *I – Is it inspring?*
> *N – Is it necessary?*
> *K – Is it kind?*

you could say: "Do you know that for sure? Have you talked to that person?" The idea is to say nice things about the person and show your friends you genuinely care about others. Otherwise, if you do not try to defend the person, you are essentially agreeing with what is said, which makes you no better than the actual gossipers.

3. Change the Subject

Let's face it: we're human, and it's hard to resist some juicy gossip sometimes. If you find yourself slowly being drawn into some gossip that others are sharing, avoid saying or listening to something you will regret by simply changing the subject. If you are subtle, then the others won't know what hit them, and they will quickly forget that they were even talking about someone. If the others continue to gossip even after you change the topic, then you could leave the room and return when they begin talking about something else.

> *Gossip ...*
> *· centers on faults.*
> *· is blind to good qualities.*
> *· is often untrue.*
> *· can't be taken back.*
> *· cuts us off from God and other people.*

If they ask you why you left, calmly explain that you don't feel comfortable talking about the person or situation or that you believe you're being disrespectful. Don't criticize them for what they are saying, but show them through your example that it is not the correct thing to do. If they are truly your friends, they will respect your decision and not give you a hard time about it. If you maintain this no-gossip stance, you may eventually influence your friends to avoid gossiping as well.

4. Put Yourself in the Victim's Place

Another way to avoid gossip is to put yourself in the place of the one being gossiped about. In chapter 2, we discussed the importance of thinking before we speak. Before you gossip, think about what you are wanting to say. Is it really necessary? How will the person feel if he or she finds out? How would you feel if others were saying such things about you? If you are only going to make someone upset by what you are wanting to say, then don't say it.

Which of the four strategies for avoiding gossip do you think would be most effective, and why?

_____

_____

_____

What are some other ideas for how you can avoid gossip?

_____

_____

_____

What will you do the next time you hear some friends start to talk badly about someone behind the person's back?

_____

_____

_____

A Time to Take Action

Just because the people around you are the ones gossiping does not excuse you from taking action. You might think that if you listen you are not doing anything wrong, but listening to the gossip makes you just as much a participant as anyone else. I know from experience that sometimes we can just be sitting alone doing nothing wrong and others suddenly flock to us as if we had a "tell me everything" sign plastered to our foreheads. I also know how difficult it is to escape these situations; we don't want to be rude, and sometimes we believe we have no choice but to listen.

But the important thing to remember when this happens is to maintain our integrity. We should make every possible attempt to show that we're not interested – whether it be by continuing our work quietly, defending the person who is being talked about, or simply stating that we're uncomfortable talking about the person. If we don't make these attempts, we become one of the gossipers instead of one of the peacemakers.

Practice What You Speak

Group Activity: Gossip Tellers
(aka Telephone)

 Purpose:

To understand how quickly gossip spreads and how different our words become each time another person repeats what we say.

 Instructions:

Sit in a circle. One person will whisper a secret message into the ear of the person sitting next to her. Each girl will take turns whispering the message she hears until it passes all around the circle. The last person will have to say what she heard, and most likely it will be very different from the original message.

ALWAYS BE HONEST

Abraham Lincoln once said, "No man has a good enough memory to make a successful liar."
What do you think he meant when he said this?

_____

_____

The more that people lie, the more inventive they become, and the more people they deceive in the process. Then, they have to constantly jog their memory to remember which lies they have told. Sometimes they even make up new lies to cover up the old ones.

Like gossiping, we know that lying is wrong, yet we have a natural tendency to do it anyway. Can you think of a time when you felt pleased that someone lied to you? Probably not. Ephesians 4:25 says, "Therefore, putting away lying, 'Let each one of you speak truth with his neighbor,' for we are members of one another." "Putting away lying" means to stop lying, and the Bible consistently uses the word "neighbor" to refer to any person – not just the person living next door to us.

Elizabeth Jimenez

Paul did not write "put away lying when you're with your friends" or "put away lying when you are being mean to others"; instead, he urged the Ephesian Christians to be honest with all people at all times. Likewise, we find these words in Colossians 3:9: "Do not lie to one another, since you have put off the old man with his deeds." Many people believe lying is okay as long as you don't do it all the time. As Christians, we need to set ourselves apart from those in the world by our unwavering honesty. If you lied a lot before you were baptized, you buried the bad habit in the water — and you should not allow it to resurface.

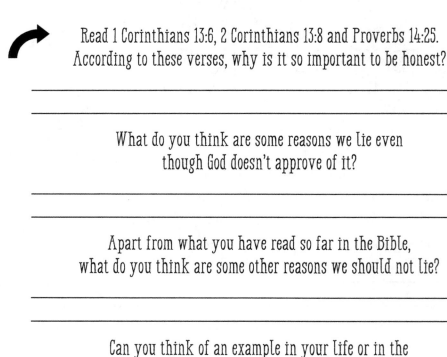

Read 1 Corinthians 13:6, 2 Corinthians 13:8 and Proverbs 14:25. According to these verses, why is it so important to be honest?

_____

_____

What do you think are some reasons we lie even though God doesn't approve of it?

_____

_____

Apart from what you have read so far in the Bible, what do you think are some other reasons we should not lie?

_____

_____

Can you think of an example in your life or in the media when someone lied to get his or her way?

_____

_____

Why Do We Lie?

Once we understand what causes us to lie, it will be much easier to control those lies, and we can save ourselves from a mountain of troubles. There are at least five key reasons why we lie, some of which can overlap.

1. To Get Our Way

When my nephew was younger, he loved to play board games. He also loved to win. Sometimes when we played together, he would say it was his turn even though he knew it wasn't or that his playing piece was really on the space but fell off or that he rolled a 10 when he really rolled a one or any other lie that would help him win the game. He was lying to get his way.

A few years ago, I really loved watching Marion Jones sprint down the track, and I admired her determination when she vowed to win five medals in the Olympics. When the Olympics committee began to investigate some suspicious accusations, she adamantly denied that she ever used any performance-enhancing drugs. Then, after two years of her lies, she tested positive for steroids, was suspended from track and field, and had to relinquish her prized medals. Imagine how disappointed I was to learn that my favorite athlete was not only a phony but that she had also lied to the world without remorse – all for the sake of winning a competition. Now that I understand what kind of person she is, I would respect her more if she had simply been honest – even if she had finished in last place.

My nephew's way was not to play fair or follow the rules. Marion Jones' way was to take drugs, win the medals illegally, and lie. God's way is to admit when we fail (rather than deny it), to lose gracefully, and to speak honestly. So many of us lie because we're only thinking about what's best for us rather than what is correct. When we lie to get our way, rather than play by God's rules, we will surely lose.

"When in doubt, tell the truth." – Unknown

2. To Please Others

Sometimes our friends pressure us, and we give in to avoid looking "uncool." For instance, a group of middle school girls hop a ride with a teenage boy and leave for the last half of the school day. They return to school just before their parents arrive to take them home. When their parents later ask if they left school, they lie, "No, of course not." They are more concerned with pleasing their friends than their parents.

The last people we should lie to are our own family members. Normally when friends pressure us, it's to do something our parents would not agree with. When our parents find out, we have two choices: tell the truth about our actions or lie. Those who lie have this kind of mentality: "When my friends find out that I lied, they will think that I am cool and will want to spend more time around me." If you are the kind of person who has to lie just to be deemed acceptable by your friends, then you have not chosen the right kind of friends. Which is worse: lying to our families and causing them to feel hurt and disappointed when they find out the truth or humbly speaking the truth and receiving their forgiveness? Obviously we should govern our words by speaking the truth with love rather than allowing peers to govern our words for us.

At times we lie to please those who are older. For example, in a job interview we might find it easier to lie and say "Yes, I have experience in this kind of job" than to admit that we know nothing about it. We might lie to our favorite teacher about what score we got on the ACT because we don't want to look bad and disappoint her. If we lie to please others, then we are not being ourselves. If we are not being ourselves, then others will have a false view of who we really are. Rather than trying to make yourself look better than you actually are, admit that you have faults and that you have made mistakes. Those who are willing to accept you for who you really are, knowing your faults and mistakes, are the ones truly worth trying to please.

3. To Protect Others

Think of a time when one of your friends was in a difficult situation and you felt compelled to stretch the truth just a little to keep him or her from getting in trouble. For example, your best friend is skipping class. When the teacher asks where she is, you say, "She's sick today." Perhaps, in your mind, you've done nothing wrong because you are sticking up for a friend. After all, if you hadn't told a lie, your friend would have been punished – not to mention she would have been really angry with you.

But in God's mind, there are no exceptions to the commandments that tell us over and over again not to lie; certainly no command says, "If your friend is in trouble, you can lie to bail her out." It's noble to protect others, but not to the point that we have to lie to do so. If you are in a situation like the one described, a better answer than lying would be "You need to

> **Deceit (noun):** dishonest behavior; behavior that is meant to fool or trick someone [7]

ask her about that" or "I don't feel comfortable talking about that" or "I would not want to answer for her." You have not said anything to accuse your friend, but you have not told a lie either.

4. To Deceive Others

Read Psalm 34:12–13 and 1 Peter 3:10.
What does the Bible say about deceit?

_____

_____

What do you think is the difference between lies and deceit?

_____

What is the cruelest joke anyone has ever played on you?

_____

How did you feel once you realized you had been deceived?

_____

_____

Another word for deceit is trickery; we trick someone into believing something. When we lie, we intentionally say something we know is not true; when we deceive, we may speak the truth but twist the words. Both are dangerous because they mislead others, and both are sinful. Some people like to trick and deceive just for fun or as part of their personality. Even those with this kind of personality, however, should consider the consequences of their actions and the effect they might have on others.

We can also deceive others without saying anything at all. Read Genesis 37:31-34. Joseph's brothers were very clever. They didn't lie, because they never actually told their father, Jacob, what happened; instead, they deceived Jacob by letting him look at the coat and form his own conclusions: "A wild beast has devoured him. Without doubt Joseph is torn to pieces" (v. 33).

Likely, Jacob struggled to love and trust his sons after he finally discovered the truth about Joseph. Our parents will also be disappointed in us and have a harder time trusting us if we deceive them.

5. To Receive Personal Gain

The best example of lying to receive personal gain is the story of Ananias and Sapphira. Read their story in Acts 5:1-11.

1. What was the specific sin of Ananias and Sapphira?

2. Whom did Peter say Ananias had lied to?

3. What happened to Ananias and Sapphira as a result of their lies?

We need to remember that when we lie, as when we gossip, there's a good chance others will eventually find out the truth. Ananias certainly never expected Peter to find out about his crime, or he probably never would have done it. But even if no one else ever finds out about our lies, God always knows. If we do not speak the truth, He will punish us – just as He did to Ananias and Sapphira.

Some students are so set on making a certain grade that they will cheat on a test, then lie when the teacher asks them about it. Others will plagiarize their research papers and essays, then insist "I wrote it. These are all my ideas." If the teacher confronts them in these situations, the students might make up a long story about how they obtained the same answers on the test or the same words in their paper because they mistakenly believe that they will improve their chances of going unpunished. Most likely, however, the teacher will quickly see through their lies and end any chance of them receiving a good grade. So many lies – only for them to be discovered, punished and no better off than before.

Can you think of a time when you lied to receive personal gain? What were the consequences?

_____

_____

_____

_____

Why We Shouldn't Lie

Many of the reasons we should not lie are the same reasons we should not gossip.

Lying Hurts Relationships

As mentioned in the example of Joseph, parents will likely have trouble trusting us if they find out we have lied to them. They will also likely feel disappointed in us and lose respect for us. The same is true for our friends and even for those we don't know very well. Think of a time you found out someone close to you had lied to you. Was it easy for you to trust that person afterward? Probably not. Some of us may have even lost friends because of one lie someone told.

Read Psalm 109:1-3. David lamented that others had lied to him and deceived him – not his friends or family or someone close to him, but "the wicked." Even so, David felt worried and depressed; perhaps he thought the only person he could trust at that point was God. If it grieved David so much that wicked people had lied to him, just imagine how much more it would have hurt had it been someone close to him. If we speak with lies and deceit, others will likely flee from us; but if we speak the truth with love, they will draw near to us.

It's Hard to Believe a Liar

Some people lie so much that even when they're telling the truth, people don't believe them. Once, a friend of mine, Angela, received an email from someone while she was out of the country telling her that her car had been totaled. Because the person who sent the email liked to joke around and trick people a lot, Angela didn't believe the message at first, assuming it was just another silly prank. Two or three days later, Angela learned that her car had, in fact, been totaled.

It's okay to joke around sometimes, but not so much that others fail to believe us in times of crisis. The more lies we tell, the less likely others will be to take us seriously – and to want to spend time around us. I certainly don't want to spend a lot of time around someone who prefers to tell vivid, made-up stories than to share what's really happening in his or her life. If you want others to take you seriously, the first step is consistent honesty.

All Lies Are Equally Sinful

We've all heard of "white lies" – you know, lies that are not so big and don't seem to cause as many problems, so they are okay (or so we think). But God does not differentiate among lies. No place in the Bible says some lies are bigger than others or some lies are more acceptable than others or some situations call for lies. It simply says, "Do not lie."

 ## Write Leviticus 19:11 in the space provided:

_____

_____

_____

Do not lie. God could not have made it any simpler for us. Don't waste your time trying to classify your lies into groups of severity or justify why some lies you told were okay. If we lie, we sin. Period. No matter what the situation is, it's always better to tell the truth.

> "These six things the Lord hates, yes, seven are an abomination to Him: a proud look, a lying tongue, hands that shed innocent blood, a heart that devises wicked plans, feet that are swift in running to evil, a false witness who speaks lies, and one who sows discord among brethren" (Proverbs 6:16-19).

Liars Will Be Punished

We already discussed some of the many negative consequences of lying: you may lose people's trust, lose relationships, or even lose your self-respect. But remember that God always knows when we lie even when others don't, and He will have a punishment reserved for us as well. In the Old Testament, God warned us, "The mouth of those who speak lies shall be stopped" (Psalm 63:11). Now, under the new law, it's clearer what "shall be stopped" refers to. Revelation 21:8 says, "But the cowardly, unbelieving, abominable, murderers, sexually immoral, sorcerers, idolaters, and all liars shall have their part in the lake which burns with fire and brimstone, which is the second death." No one could doubt from these verses that God dislikes liars and that those who do not repent of their lies will have no place in heaven. Is any lie worth the risk of losing our salvation?

A Time to Choose

How can you tell when someone is lying to you?

_____

_____

What should you do if you find out a friend has told you a lie?

_____

_____

How important is it to you that your friends be honest? why?

_____

_____

How is lying similar to gossiping? How are they different?

_____

_____

When it comes to lying, we have two examples to follow: God's or Satan's. John 8:44 describes Satan as the father of all lies. He "does not stand in the truth," it says, "because there is no truth in him. When he speaks a lie, he speaks from his own resources, for he is a liar and the father of it." Would you like to be told that "you are of your father the devil"? In other words, you do not speak the truth as your father the devil does not speak the truth. What harsh words to hear.

God, on the other hand, is full of truth. Hebrews 6:18 says, "It is impossible for God to lie." Sometimes we think that as long as we're honest 90 percent of the time, we're on the right track. We might be on the right track, but we are not following God's example until we are honest 100 percent of the time. Wouldn't it be better to hear others say we follow God's example and are honest than to hear them say we follow Satan's example and are dishonest? Starting today, make a pact with yourself to stop speaking dishonestly or deceitfully and to speak only the truth.

Practice What You Speak
Individual Challenge: Scripture Defense

 Purpose:

To follow what the Bible says about honesty rather than telling a lie.

 Instructions:

Memorize three different verses about lying or honesty. They can be verses that were included in the chapter or any others that interest you. Try to learn a new verse each week for three weeks. The next time you are tempted to tell a lie, quote one or all of the verses in your head. Hopefully this small act will go a long way in helping you to be more honest.

Group Activity: Two Truths and a Lie

 Purpose:

To get to know one another better and to understand how difficult it can be to distinguish lies from the truth.

 Instructions:

Each girl should take a turn telling two sentences that are true about herself and one that is not true. Then the other girls should vote on which sentence they believe is the lie.

Chapter 10

CONTROL YOUR ANGER

*W*hen I was younger, I used to yell, slam doors, and stomp up the stairs anytime I was angry. Basically I wanted everyone around me to know I was mad and to not get in my way. It is not a sin to be angry. It's the way we are made, and even God and Jesus get angry at times. But if we don't control our anger, it can lead to sins such as hatred and strife. It can also cause others to be angry at us. We need to demonstrate an attitude of peace and acceptance and try not to let our anger get out of control.

What the Bible Says About Anger

Read the following five verses about anger, and write the missing words for each one.

1. Proverbs 21:19: "Better to dwell in the _____, than with a _____ and _____ woman."

2. Proverbs 22:24: "Make no _____ with an _____ man, and with a _____ man do not go."

3. Psalm 37:8: "Cease from _____, and forsake _____."

4. Ephesians 4:31: "Let all _____, _____, _____, _____, and _____ _____ be put away from you, with all malice."

5. Titus 1:7: "For a bishop must be blameless, as a steward of God, not
_____, not _____, not given to wine, not
_____, not greedy for money."

> *"Anger is a feeling that makes your mouth*
> *work faster than your mind."*
> *— Unknown*

Be Slow to Anger

If we don't control our tongues when we are angry, we tend to raise our voices and yell at anyone – even if it's not that person's fault. The Bible clearly instructs us to be slow to anger. If we take a minute to calm ourselves down the instant we feel angry, then we may be able to prevent yelling or blaming others. Proverbs 16:32 says, "He who is slow to anger is better than the mighty, and he who rules his spirit than he who takes a city." Most people don't want to be around someone who blows up in anger all the time. God is also slow to anger, as we find in Psalm 145:8: "The LORD is gracious and full of compassion, slow to anger and great in mercy."

When we react slowly to our anger, we demonstrate self-control – a fruit of the Spirit (Galatians 5:22-23) – and others will value us more for our self-discipline. James 1:19 tells us, "So then, my beloved brethren, let every man be swift to hear, slow to speak, slow to wrath." As we have already learned, we should listen attentively when others tell us something, choose our words very carefully, and avoid showing our anger. Finally, in Proverbs 19:11, we find that "the discretion of a man makes him slow to anger, and his glory is to overlook a transgression." Do you want to be considered wise? If so, do not let yourself get angry so easily, and learn to control your anger before it controls you.

Avoid Going to Bed Angry

According to Ephesians 4:26, you should not "let the sun go down on your wrath." If you are in a bad mood, try to resolve the issue before you go to bed; otherwise, you will wake up with the same feelings of anger and resentment the next day – if you're even able to sleep. Anger and forgiveness go hand in hand. Just as we need to approach others and ask for their forgiveness when we've done something wrong, there may be times when we need to approach those who have angered us and explain how we feel. Many times the person did not make us angry intentionally, and if we simply take the time to clear up any confusion and misunderstandings as soon as possible, we can save both ourselves and the other person a lot of pain and resentment later.

Anger Leads to Danger

When was a time your anger led you to do something you shouldn't have done?

_____

_____

What would have been a better way for you to react in that situation?

_____

_____

Matthew 5:22 states, "But I say to you that whoever is angry with his brother without a cause shall be in danger of the judgment." We especially should avoid showing too much anger with our family members – including those of the church. Otherwise, we could lose our salvation, as with all the other matters of failing to control our tongues. What a shame that some Christians so frequently stop coming to church just because of some anger they feel toward others in the church or because of something minor that happened at one church service. No matter how great your anger may seem, don't allow it to interfere with your spirituality – much less with the spirituality of others.

Habits to Avoid

If left uncontrolled, anger can lead to arguments and disagreements – sometimes even grudges. Proverbs 15:18 says, "A wrathful man stirs up strife, but he who is slow to anger allays contention." If we get angry easily, we might have problems with others, but if we control our anger, we can avoid these problems.

{ _"An angry man stirs up strife, and a furious man abounds in transgression"_ (Proverbs 29:22). }

105

Elizabeth Jimenez

Avoid Unnecessary Arguments

In order to have healthy, unified relationships with others, we should avoid unnecessary arguments and disagreements. Paul told Titus to "avoid foolish disputes, genealogies, contentions, and strivings about the law; for they are unprofitable and useless" (Titus 3:9). Also, Paul urged the brethren in 1 Corinthians 1:10, "Now I plead with you, brethren, by the name of our Lord Jesus Christ, that you all speak the same thing, and that there be no divisions among you, but that you be perfectly joined together in the same mind and in the same judgment."

Certainly, unnecessary disagreements bring about unwanted divisions with our friends, co-workers, family members and fellow Christians. These disagreements can also prevent unity, which is so critical to church growth and our personal faith. It's okay to be angry, and it's okay to disagree with someone, but if we are not careful about what we say, the disagreement could change our relationship with that person forever. When we feel angry, we need to find a way to channel our anger so others are not negatively affected by our bad attitudes. We could go to our rooms and close the door, pray, read the Bible, practice a hobby, exercise, or anything else that helps take our minds off what happened and gets us away from others until we can think rationally again.

Abram understood exactly how to choose his words in order to avoid unnecessary disagreements. When he and Lot had to decide which land to move to, he purposefully let Lot choose first, as we find in Genesis 13:8: "So Abram said to Lot, 'Please let there be no strife between you and me, and between my herdsmen and your herdsmen; for we are brethren.' " Are you the kind of person who is constantly arguing or causing conflicts? If so, then you will have a hard time keeping friends. If you are always reserved and don't try to stir up others with your words, they will respect you more and may even come to you when they are having problems.

> What is the difference between arguments and unnecessary arguments? Can you think of a time when you shouldn't avoid conflict?

_____

_____

_____

Avoid Fighting Words

Anger can also drive us to fight if we're not careful. According to Proverbs 17:14,

"The beginning of strife is like releasing water; therefore stop contention before a quarrel starts." Have you ever watched two people get into each other's faces and start yelling and fighting verbally – all because of something one of them said that the other didn't like? I have, and unfortunately, it ended in physical fighting as well, with both people receiving major cuts and bruises and getting suspended from school.

Write Proverbs 20:3 in the space provided:

_____

_____

_____

Oftentimes those who try to start quarrels act macho, but secretly they suffer from low self-esteem; they think that attacking others will make them feel better about themselves. I once had a student who responded to insults by attacking back with even harsher words. She yelled "Don't you talk about me!" so aggressively that the other person had no choice but to back down. Why? Because she thought this was the best way to defend herself. As a result of constant teasing, her self-esteem suffered, and she thought her aggressive behavior would somehow make her seem more powerful than the others. What she didn't realize was that everyone in the class was secretly laughing and saying even more mean things about her every time this happened. Her fighting words only made her more disliked by her classmates, rather than more valued.

Those who ignore contentions, however, have much more confidence, and they don't need others to tell them who's right and who's wrong because they believe in themselves. A better defense, and the one God approves of, is to refrain from saying anything that would cause others to talk badly about us in the first place. If we mind our own business and don't bother others with our words, they will have no reason to bother us.

Habits to Adopt

Seek Reconciliation, Not Revenge

No matter what someone else does to you, trying to get that person back will only make matters worse. Whatever we try to do as revenge will likely be another sin. So, instead, we need to trust in God to take care of those situations for us, as we are told in Romans 12:19: "Beloved, do not avenge yourselves, but rather give place to wrath; for it is written, 'Vengeance is Mine, I will repay,' says the Lord."

We should also strive to forgive the person, as we would want him or her to forgive us. First Peter 3:8-9 says:

> Finally, all of you be of one mind, having compassion for one another; love as brothers, be tenderhearted, be courteous; not returning evil for evil or reviling for reviling, but on the contrary blessing, knowing that you were called to this, that you may inherit a blessing.

Seeking revenge will only put us on others' – and God's – bad side, but seeking reconciliation will help us – and the ones who made us angry – experience closure and peace of mind.

Choose Your Words Carefully

Whatever our anger leads us to say, we will not be able to take those words back afterward. Then, when we have to pay the consequences for our angry words, we become even angrier.

Once a student received in-school suspension as a punishment for skipping class. He was so angry when he found out that he cursed his teacher to her face, getting himself kicked out of school for two months. Once his anger subsided and he realized the foolishness of his actions, he immediately wished to take his words back. He confessed to the teacher: "I don't think I should be kicked out of school, because I never did anything like that before. This was the first time, and look what happened." Unfortunately, it doesn't matter if it's the first time or the hundredth time; when you say something stupid out of anger, you will have to pay the consequences.

Turn Your Anger Into Something Good

Although Moses became angry easily, he did not allow his anger to turn into sin. Instead, he used his anger to prevent the Israelites from sinning. In Exodus 32, Moses had just returned from Mount Sinai when he saw that the Israelites had made a golden calf to worship. At first he did not control his anger very well, breaking the tablets and burning the golden calf in the fire. Then he started thinking more rationally, pleading with the Israelites to join him on the Lord's side.

Although Moses was angry, he insisted that the Israelites turn from their wrong ways and even spoke to the Lord on their behalf: "Then Moses returned to the LORD and said, 'Oh, these people have committed a great sin, and have made for themselves a god of gold! Yet now, if You will forgive their sin – but if not, I pray, blot me out of Your book which You have written' " (Exodus 32:31-32). Most of us would have returned to our tents like nothing happened or yelled at the Israelites out of rage, but Moses had the courage to keep following God despite his anger and was even humble enough to take the blame for their downfall. When we become angry, let's follow Moses' example and turn our anger into something good for others rather than something that will cause them to stumble. Most important, let's not allow our anger to become so great that it causes us to sin.

A Time for Control

The next time someone makes you angry, don't just fly off the handle, hurling insults and complaints. Instead, try to control yourself. Go to a quiet place where you can be alone, if it's necessary. Avoid saying anything that will cause either of you to feel angrier; in fact, just by refraining from negative words, you can be encouraging. Also remember not to exaggerate something small into a big problem.

Rather than allowing our anger to control us and cause us to sin or have strife with others, we should strive to turn our anger into something that will make a positive difference. With our tongues we have the power to create conflict or prevent conflict. Which will you choose?

Practice What You Speak
Individual Challenge: Anger Journal

 Purpose:

To write the angry words we want to say instead of expressing them verbally.

 Instructions:

One way you can channel your anger without affecting others is to write down everything you are feeling in that moment. Actually, I have written some of my best poems when I felt most angry. Keep an "anger journal," and write down what makes you mad and why. Try to write in your journal as soon as possible while your emotions are still fresh and before you have a chance to yell or argue with others.

Group Activity: Bowl O' Anger

 Purpose:

To discuss how to control our anger in different situations and/or experience a more peaceful resolution.

 Instructions:

Each girl should write down a time she felt particularly angry and experienced unfavorable consequences as a result. She should not write her name on her paper, leaving her response anonymous. The girls should fold their papers and put them in a bowl; then, they can take turns pulling out the papers and reading them aloud. Discuss as a group (or in smaller groups) what each person should have done in response to her anger or what she could have done to turn her anger into something good. Try not to use vague answers such as "She should have controlled her anger." Instead, think carefully about what should have been done in that situation and provide specific ideas. For example, if a girl writes that she felt angry with her teacher, one idea would be for her to talk to her teacher in private and explain why she felt that way.

PRACTICE SILENCE, PART 1

*A*ccording to the philosopher William Penn, "True silence is the rest of the mind, and is to the spirit what sleep is to the body, nourishment and refreshment. It is a great virtue: it covers folly, keeps secrets, avoids disputes, and prevents sin." So far we have learned what we should say or should avoid saying in order to control our tongues. Now we will examine some times we can control our tongues simply by not saying anything. In chapter 2, we referred to Ecclesiastes 3:1, where Solomon said, "To everything there is a season, a time for every purpose under heaven." Then we find, "A time to tear, and a time to sew; a time to keep silence, and a time to speak" (v. 7).

When are some times we should keep silent?

_____

_____

When are some times we should speak?

_____

_____

The Times We Should Keep Silent

When Older People Talk to Us

Any time another person talks to us, we should listen and try not to interrupt, but especially when the person is older. First Peter 5:5 says, "Likewise you younger people, submit yourselves to your elders. Yes, all of you be submissive to one another." In this verse, an "elder" doesn't just mean an elder in the church; it could be a teacher, a grandparent, a friend's mom or anyone else who is older than you.

What does it mean to "submit yourselves to your elders"?

_____

_____

Submit (verb):
to stop trying to fight or resist something; to agree to do or accept something that you have been resisting or opposing [8]

Our elders often have more wisdom and authority than we do, and even though the stories they tell may seem long and old-fashioned, we can learn a lot from their experiences. But first we have to submit to them by listening respectfully and giving them the attention they deserve. The next time your friends tempt you to talk during class or make fun of an old man for the way he rambles on, remember that this older person has more to say than you do and just might be sharing something very important. We need to respect our elders when they speak by not talking at the same time, laughing or interrupting.

Read through this list of Moses' excuses in modern terms.
Do any sound like excuses you have made or heard in the past?

- I don't have any experience.
- I don't want them to get mad at me.
- What if they don't believe me?

_____

_____

_____

What should we offer God instead of excuses?

_____

_____

When We Feel Like Making Excuses

When someone asks you to do something that you're not too excited about, what's the first thing you do? Most of us make excuses to get out of it. Your mom asks you to empty the dishwasher, and you say you have too much homework. Your teacher asks you to stay after school for a special project, and you say you have to go to help your mom do laundry. Normally these excuses accomplish nothing more than to free us of responsibility. When we don't make excuses, however, we sometimes find that the responsibility is not as difficult as we thought it would be. If we would stop wasting time making excuses and just do what we're asked, then we would be more productive – and help others at the same time. We might even discover a new talent or opportunity that would have never existed otherwise.

One person from the Bible who made a lot of excuses was Moses. At first he did not want to be the leader of the Israelites, because he was afraid of appearing before Pharaoh and being in charge of such a large group of people. When he finally stopped making excuses, however, God used him to become a great leader that the people admired and depended on. Read about this story in Exodus 3:1–4:20, and answer the questions that follow.

1. What excuses did Moses make in each of the following verses to try to get out of returning to Egypt?

• Exodus 3:11:

• Exodus 3:13:

• Exodus 4:1:

• Exodus 4:10:

• Exodus 4:13:

2. How did God react to Moses' many excuses?

3. How do you think God feels when we make excuses instead of doing what He or others need us to do?

Just imagine what would have happened to the Israelites if Moses had continued making excuses instead of doing this important job. We can make excuses all day long, but if something needs to be done or someone needs help, the excuses will not make the responsibility any less necessary.

Most of the time when we make excuses, we act selfishly rather than putting others before ourselves. We think "I don't have time" or "I don't know how" or "I am not the right person to do this" or "I already helped a lot." Or, like Moses, we simply think, "Why me?" Instead of worrying so much about our personal needs, what we should be thinking is "The other person needs my help. The other person can't do this job alone. The other person values my skills and abilities." If we think the work is too hard or we're not qualified, we should trust in God to guide us as Moses learned to do.

Another reason we shouldn't make excuses is because doing so lets others down. Like lies and hypocrisy, it's not hard to detect when someone is saying something just to get out of doing a job.

 ## When was a time you let someone down by making excuses?

_____

_____

 ## What should you have done instead?

_____

_____

A time will come when you will need someone to help you with something. When that happens, the ones you have helped when they needed it will likely be more than glad to return the favor. But those you have let down will likely do the same to you when you need help the most. Making excuses to avoid difficult situations accomplishes nothing, but keeping our mouths shut and simply doing what we're asked to do can produce stronger bonds with others and provide greater opportunities.

When We Feel Like Complaining

As with excuses, those who complain accomplish nothing but to bring negative attention to themselves. Jude 16 explains, "Grumblers, complainers, [walk] according to their own lusts; and they mouth great swelling words, flattering people to gain advantage."

1. What do you think "walking according to their own lusts" means?

2. How do you feel when you are around someone who acts this way?

• *Complaints of the Scribes and Pharisees*

Two groups of people who complained a lot to "gain advantage" were the scribes and Pharisees. They complained about what people did that went against their teachings in hopes of pointing out Jesus' faults and making Him look foolish. In the end, they were the ones who always looked foolish, for Jesus consistently proved them wrong. Their complaints did not help them fulfill their purpose; on the contrary, they served only to reaffirm Jesus' power. The people might have respected them more if they had just kept their mouths closed instead of complaining about every little thing.

• *Complaints of the Israelites*

The Israelites also complained a lot – so much so that God grew angry with them. Read the following passages, and write what the Israelites complained about each time.

1. Exodus 16:2-3:

2. Exodus 17:3:

3. Numbers 14:1-5:

What happened in these verses when God became angry with the Israelites' complaints?

1. Exodus 16:4-5:

2. Numbers 11:1:

3. Numbers 14:26-30:

As a result of their endless complaints, God banned the Israelites from the land of Canaan. Numbers 14:33 says, "And your sons shall be shepherds in the wilderness forty years, and bear the brunt of your infidelity, until your carcasses are consumed in the wilderness." After so much time and preparation, their hopes were dashed, and only the non-complainers – Joshua, Caleb and the children – were allowed to enter the Promised Land. The Israelites went from living a peaceful life and having God's blessings to wandering aimlessly with no guidance – all because of their complaints.

It's important to note that complaining is much different from asking for help. The Israelites never tried to speak directly to God or to Moses about their situation; they simply voiced outrage as if they deserved everything. When we have a problem, a better solution than complaining is to pray to God and ask Him to provide a solution. We could also talk privately with someone responsible for the problem, calmly explaining why we're frustrated and what we think should be done. The calmer we are when we speak, the more likely others will be to listen to us and make the necessary changes. If we raise our voices and spew out complaint after complaint, others may also grow angry and be less likely to help us.

• *Complaints of Martha*

Another biblical character who complained was Martha. Feeling frustrated that her sister, Mary, was not helping her in the kitchen, she exclaimed to Jesus: "Lord, do You not care that my sister has left me to serve alone? Therefore tell her to help me" (Luke 10:40). We have probably all felt like Martha at times – having so much to do and no one to help us do it. Again, the better option in these situations is to keep our mouths closed and get the work done or politely and calmly ask another person to help us. If we complain, we will cause the others to think that we are selfish and whiny; no one wants to help someone who acts like that. Jesus' response to Martha was simply not to worry (v. 41). Like the Israelites, she was sweating the small stuff instead of appreciating the great things.

 ## Write Philippians 2:14–15 in the space provided:

_____

_____

_____

When those around us are complaining, we need to be careful not to let their attitudes rub off on us, and we need to let our lights shine by not complaining.

The next time you're frustrated about something, try not to complain out loud and receive negative attention. Instead, keep your thoughts to yourself until an opportunity arises for you to take action. As when someone asks us to do something, we can solve the problem a lot faster when we work rather than when we complain.

When We Feel Proud

Several verses in the Bible emphasize that those who are too proud will be punished. In fact, boasters fall on the list of those "deserving of death" in Romans 1:29-32. Read the following verses, and fill in the missing words for each one.

1. James 4:16: "You boast in your _____. All such boasting is _____."

2. Jeremiah 50:31-32: " 'Behold, I am against you, O most _____ one!' says the Lord GOD of hosts; 'for your day has come, the time that I will _____ you. The most proud shall stumble and _____, and no one will raise him up; I will kindle a fire in his cities, and it will _____ all around him.' "

3. Proverbs 16:18: "_____ goes before _____, and a haughty spirit before a _____."

Acting too proudly only causes us to fall, meaning we will face greater problems. The further we fall with our pride, the harder it will be for others to help us back up and for us to recover from the disaster we may find ourselves in.

What letter is in the middle of the word "pride"? Instead of "I," who does God want us to focus on?

_____

_____

_____

Boasting is sinful because it takes all the attention off others and puts it on us. Have you ever known someone to boast on behalf of another person? Probably not. Most of the time when we boast we are thinking only of ourselves – "I did this" or "I'm so good at this" or "I am the best person here." Proverbs 27:2 states, "Let another man praise you, and not your own mouth; a stranger, and not your own lips." Just imagine how much more meaningful the congratulations

Elizabeth Jimenez

will be if others recognize our hard work than if we boast about it ourselves.

Another reason boasting is wrong is because it causes us to compare ourselves to others. For example, a person you know scored 20 points in the basketball game, so the day you score 22 points, you exclaim, "I scored more!" Or maybe it's not about something you do, but something you have. If you suddenly obtain more pairs of shoes than your best friend, do you want to rub it in her face?

Read 2 Corinthians 10:12–13.
What did Paul describe those who compare themselves
to others as not being?

_____

_____

If we are constantly thinking about how we compare to others, we may foolishly fall into the sins of envy, jealousy or covetousness. God made all of us different for a reason and gave us all different talents. Instead of boasting or comparing ourselves to others, we need to have a spirit of humility. First Peter 5:5 instructs us to "be clothed with humility, for 'God resists the proud, but gives grace to the humble.' "

What does it mean to "be clothed with humility"?

_____

_____

Humility (noun):
the quality or state
of not thinking you are
better than other people [9]

People who are clothed with humility are quiet and sincere. They are not boastful, and they do not try to call attention to themselves. They understand when something needs to be done, and they do it. It doesn't matter if they do it secretly with no one finding out about it, because they work hard for the benefit of others, not for themselves. Also, they do not feel a need to brag or show off because they understand that God is the One in control.

That is the most important reason why we should not boast: because, when we do, we fail to give God the credit He deserves. God is constantly watching out for us, and He makes all things possible for us – from the friends we make to the cars we drive to the clothes we wear to the points we score and everything in-between. Second Corinthians 10:17 says, "He who glories, let him glory in the LORD." If we're going to boast about something, let's boast about how wonderful, loving and understanding God is. Remember that we also learned we should thank God constantly. If you accomplish something amazing that you feel you just have to share with someone, then say a little prayer to thank God for that accomplishment. God helped in some way, and we need to acknowledge His role.

"The unspoken word never does harm." – Lajos Kossuth

A Time to Refrain

Remember that there are times to talk and times to refrain from talking. Impulsive remarks serve no purpose and may offend those who hear them. Once you recognize that you are about to interrupt, make an excuse, complain, boast or say something disrespectful, keep your comments inside your head, keep your mouth closed, and keep your attention on the other person – not on yourself.

Practice What You Speak

Group Activity: Trashed Excuses and Complaints

 Purpose:

To identify some common excuses and complaints we should "throw out" of our vocabulary.

 Instructions:

Each girl should receive two pieces of paper (preferably two different colors). On one sheet, she should write a common excuse, and on the other, a common complaint. It can be things she has said at some point or things she has heard others say. When all the girls have finished, they should sit together in a circle. One at a time, the girls should step forward to read one excuse and one complaint. Then they should wad up the papers and throw them into a trash can in the middle of the circle. This activity should remind them that we want to "throw away" all of our excuses and complaints.

Chapter 12

PRACTICE SILENCE, PART 2

*A*lthough I grew up in the church, I never really took worship seriously. Like many kids my age, I would draw pictures, sleep through the sermon, or whisper and giggle with my friends. What I looked forward to most was seeing my friends, so, at times, church felt more like a social experience than a spiritual one. Then when I got baptized, I came to understand that others were looking to me to do the right thing. Gone were the silly pictures and notes, the naps, and the extended whispered conversations, replaced by sermon notes, better listening skills, and an ever-present awareness that worship meant glorifying God with my whole heart. I wanted to honor my baptism by my actions, and I wanted to behave in a way that others would be proud to call me their new Christian sister.

Another time when it is extremely important for us to practice silence is during worship services and devotionals. And the way we act at church serves as a model for how we should act during other times of silence, such as in assemblies or ceremonies.

Why We Should Practice Silence in Worship

There are five main reasons we should maintain silence during worship services.

> "Praise the Lord! I will praise the Lord with my whole heart, in the assembly of the upright and in the congregation" (Psalm 111:1).

1. To Honor God

The first reason we need to maintain silence during worship is to honor God.

 Write 1 Peter 2:17 in the space provided, and answer the questions that follow.

_____

_____

_____

 What do you think it means to fear God and honor the king?

_____

_____

 The verse also says to "honor all people." What are some ways we honor others?

_____

_____

Usually when we read in the Bible that we should "fear God," it means we should honor and revere Him and acknowledge Him as loving and powerful. If we are talking, laughing or acting inappropriately during worship services, we are not showing God the respect He deserves, nor are we respecting the men participating in the service.

One way we honor others is by celebrating special days in their memory. For example, we honor veterans by remembering them on Veterans Day. God also has a special day set aside for us to honor Him, and that is Sunday. We show respect on His special day by listening and not talking during worship. We can also honor someone with gifts or compliments. Some of the gifts we use to honor God in worship include singing, praying and teaching or preaching – all of which are excellent ways to use our tongues.

124

One of the gifts, singing, is definitely a part of worship during which we should not be silent. Even if you don't have the greatest voice, singing out and risking the embarrassment is better than not singing at all. We should sing from our hearts as we are instructed in Ephesians 5:19: "[Speak] to one another in psalms and hymns and spiritual songs, singing and making melody in your heart to the Lord." When others see us singing, they will know we love God and want to act appropriately. Older folks especially feel encouraged when they hear young people singing to God.

Maybe you do sing, but your mind wanders during the song. As you sing, try to focus on the words of each song – what the words mean and how they can influence your life for the better. If you start to sing more during church or think more seriously about the words of the hymns, you will honor God through your praise, and your spirituality will quickly grow.

Tips for worship etiquette:

• You should enter worship services before they begin (instead of walking in late).

• If you need to leave during worship (to use the bathroom, for example), you should wait until an appropriate time.

• You should only talk in worship while praising God.

What other tip(s) can you think of?

_____

_____

_____

2. To Respect Our Leaders

Just as we should honor God by listening quietly, we should also honor the men who lead us in worship. Imagine that you are teaching a children's class and everyone in the class is talking and laughing as if you weren't even there. You're trying desperately to teach them the Bible story, but no matter what you try, the kids refuse to listen. Now you know exactly how those who participate in the worship service feel when they see you talking or looking away. Sometimes we kid ourselves into thinking they don't notice, but they do.

Once a man accidentally dropped his Bible during the sermon and made his wife laugh a tiny bit, which caused the preacher to pause his sermon. The couple felt so bad about laughing, they decided to apologize to the preacher. The couple explained the reason they were laughing because they didn't want the preacher to think they were laughing at him. It took several minutes for the couple to convince the preacher they had nothing against him or his sermon.

Of course accidents do happen, but we need to be very careful not to do anything that would give our worship leaders the impression that we're disrespecting them. Just as we wouldn't want others to show us disrespect when we're trying to do a good work, we shouldn't show disrespect to others in that position either. It takes a lot of courage to stand in front of the entire congregation and lead some part of worship – whether it's reading Scripture, praying, singing or preaching. We need to put ourselves in these men's shoes and let them see that we honor them for their leadership in worship.

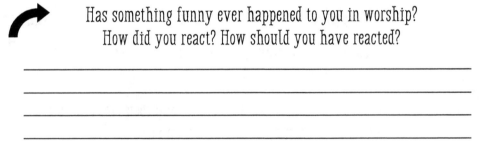

Has something funny ever happened to you in worship? How did you react? How should you have reacted?

_____

_____

_____

_____

3. To Avoid Being a Distraction

On a Wednesday night several years ago, I was sitting in the back of church with two of my friends. All eyes were focused on the preacher, who was standing in the front giving the weekly invitation. Suddenly, a baby pulled his pacifier out of his mouth and heaved it into the air. In one instant, it thudded onto the back of a man's bald head like a basketball ricocheting off a backboard. In the next instant, my friends and I were shaking in uncontrollable laughter, muffling our mouths so our sounds would not break the silence. Occasionally a strange "humph" noise escaped through our hands, and everyone close by turned to glare at us – including our mothers.

We did not do a very good job controlling our tongues. Even though we never said anything, our laughter distracted those around us and made the seriousness of the invitation seem comical.

According to Paul, worship should be done "decently and in order" (1 Corinthians 14:40). In other words, the worship service should be free of inappropriate behaviors and distractions. Many times our tongues cause these distractions. For example, if someone shouts "Amen" at the end of every sentence the preacher says, the other members may eventually start to lose focus on the sermon because they are so curious about who's saying "Amen" so much. I'm not saying that shouting "Amen" is wrong; I'm only saying that even good things we say, if done too much, can get out of order.

Just because others can't hear what we're saying, they can still become distracted just from seeing our lips moving or watching our facial expressions.

Name examples of distractions caused by our tongues. (Hint: think about how the causes can be different for different age groups.)

_____

_____

_____

"The word listen contains the same letters as the word silent." — Alfred Brendel

4. To Display Interest and Maturity

Another reason we should control our tongues during worship is so others can see we love the Lord and we take His Word seriously. If we don't refrain from using our tongues, they may think we don't have any interest in the sermon and we would rather be outside talking with our friends than sitting through another service. If you are talking while someone else is talking, what will she think? Probably that you are bored or not interested in what she has to say. God will feel the same way if we are talking or cutting up during worship. I know from experience that it's hard for young girls not to talk to one another sometimes, but just remember that whatever it is you think you need to say, it can wait. It's not as important as your heavenly Father.

Learn to wait and tell your friends whatever you need to tell them when church is over. Sometimes we have to wait more than a week without talking to our friends, so why should it be so hard to sit for an hour in church without telling them something? According to James 1:26, "If anyone among you thinks he is religious, and does not bridle his tongue but deceives his own heart, this one's religion is useless." Talking or laughing inappropriately during church is not worth the risk of others thinking our religion is useless.

One time, some teenage girls from church got together to eat and play games. The hostess was praying for the food they were about to eat when suddenly she heard one of the girls giggling. Like a chain reaction, each of the other girls in turn started laughing louder and louder, until eventually none of them could even hear what was being said in the prayer. Confused, the hostess didn't know if she should pause the prayer in the middle or just continue as if nothing happened.

This kind of behavior may be expected from young children, but not from teenage girls. First Corinthians 14:20 says: "Brethren, do not be children in understanding; however, in malice be babes, but in understanding be mature."

What does it mean to you to be mature?

_____

_____

To me being mature means acting our age and letting wisdom guide every decision. When we don't control our tongues during worship, we are like children: silly, unruly and immature. But if we learn to sit through worship silently, we will show others that we are truly interested in God's Word, we will demonstrate maturity and set good examples for others.

5. To Set a Good Example

Speaking of setting a good example, do you realize how many eyes are watching you in a worship service? I'm not just talking about the elders and deacons, your teachers or even your friends. I'm talking about the eyes of innocent children. How do you think children learn to sit still and listen during a church service? By observing those around them. Another group of people who might be observing you is new converts. Like children, these people sometimes need to watch others to understand what to do and what not to do.

If a child or a new Christian sees you talking or laughing during a worship service, what might he or she think about you?

_____

_____

What do you want young children and new converts
to learn from your example?

_____

_____

A Time to Be an Example

Worship is one of the main times we need to control our tongues. We honor God by paying attention during the sermon and praising Him during the prayers and songs. We also set a good example of how to act in worship for those younger or those new to the church. If we don't control our tongues during church, we become a distraction to others, making it difficult for them to receive the vital spiritual nourishment they need. Worse yet, we give the appearance of one who doesn't really care about God and comes to church only because she has to or because she wants to spend time with her friends. If you truly feel inspired by God's Word, then let others see you acting appropriately during every worship service – saving your laughter and silly comments for later.

Practice What You Speak

Individual Challenge: Sermon Notes

 ## Purpose:

To help you stay focused during worship and free yourself of the temptation to talk.

 ## Instructions:

If you have a hard time paying attention in church, try taking notes about the sermon. It will help you stay more focused and grow spiritually at the same time. It will also show others that you are serious about church and make your friends less likely to tempt you to talk.

PURIFY YOUR SPEECH

*I*n Matthew 15, the scribes and Pharisees tried to test Jesus by asking why the disciples violated the hand-washing tradition. Jesus answered them, "Not what goes into the mouth defiles a man; but what comes out of the mouth, this defiles a man" (v. 11). Jesus often taught about the importance of having a pure mouth, and later His apostles continued these teachings. We cannot control what the people around us say, but we can control what we say. And if we spend a lot of time around people who misuse their tongues, we should be careful not to allow them to defile us from the inside.

Name some impurities that come out of our mouths and defile us.

_____

_____

We can sum up everything from the previous chapters by saying we need to speak with purity. If we refrain from gossip, lies, excuses, complaints, anger and insults and if we use our mouths for uplifting others through encouraging words, evangelism and thankfulness, our mouths will be pure – just as God intended for them to be. Before we say something, we need to ask, is this pure? Will others appreciate what I'm about to say? Or will they be offended by it or ashamed of me? Hopefully others will know we are trying to please God just by the way we speak.

> *What do we use to clean our bodies? Soap, right?*
> *So what can we use to clean our spirits? Dove soap.*
> *In other words, the Holy Spirit (who appeared as a dove).[10]*
> *Think about this every time you see or use a Dove product*
> *— God is cleansing you from within.*

What Does It Mean to Speak With Purity?

So what does it mean to speak with purity? Let's see what the Bible has to say on the subject.

To Speak From the Heart

Fill in the blanks for the following verses, and answer the prompts that follow.

1. Matthew 12:34: "Brood of _____! How can you, being _____, speak _____ things? For out of the abundance of the _____ the mouth _____."

2. Luke 6:45: "A _____ man out of the _____ treasure of his _____ brings forth _____; and an _____ man out of the _____ treasure of his _____ brings forth _____. For out of the abundance of the _____ his mouth _____."

3. If our hearts are evil, we will speak _____.

4. If our hearts are good, we will speak _____.

Anytime we feel very strongly about something, let's speak boldly about it rather than keeping it only to ourselves. If we have pure thoughts in our hearts, then whatever comes out of our mouths will be pure also and bring about good results. Otherwise, it's better to keep our thoughts to ourselves.

To Speak Healthy Words

Fill in the blanks for the following verse, and answer the questions that follow.

1. Proverbs 15:4: "A wholesome _____ is a tree of _____, but _____ in it breaks the _____."

2. What is another word for "wholesome"?

3. What is another word for "perverseness"?

Think of the biggest tree you have ever seen. We don't always notice the trees around us, but they provide many of our basic needs such as oxygen, shade, paper and sometimes food. Now think of a dead tree, and picture how ugly and lifeless it looks compared to a thriving one. Every time a tree loses its fruit and leaves, it looks less and less like a healthy tree. Similarly, every time we speak an unhealthy word – whether it is an insult, complaint or threat – we look less and less like a Christian. These words will break us down little by little until, like the tree, we no longer bear any fruit.

If a tree is healthy, it bears fruit that is good for everyone to eat. The same is true about our words. We should strive to say only healthy words that are okay for anyone to hear.

Name the fruit of the Spirit (Galatians 5:22-23).

_____

_____

_____

As we have already seen in previous chapters, we use our tongues to produce many of these fruits. When we speak with purity, we use our tongues to positively affect those around us. At the same time, we grow ourselves. Let's make sure that only good fruit comes from our mouths, not rotten fruit.

When was a time your tongue got you into big trouble? What did you learn from that experience?

_____

_____

_____

To Speak With Control
Fill in the blanks for the following verses.

1. Psalm 141:3: "Set a _____, O LORD, over my _____; keep watch over the door of my _____."

2. Proverbs 13:3: "He who _____ his _____ preserves his _____, but he who _____ wide his _____ shall have _____."

3. The first verse is a prayer of _____. Because he understood how difficult it is to control the tongue, he asked God to help him with this task.

4. In Proverbs 13:3, what kind of destruction do you think will come to the one who "opens wide his lips"? _____

_____

We have already mentioned in the other chapters how important it is to control our tongues. Basically, if we open our big mouths without thinking, it can get us into big trouble.

James 3:2-3 says: "For we all stumble in many things. If anyone does not stumble in word, he is a perfect man, able also to bridle the whole body. Indeed, we put bits in horses' mouths that they may obey us, and we turn their whole body." A horse that does not have a bit in its mouth roams about freely and cannot be controlled. If we fail to control our tongues, we will also find ourselves acting on our desires and making bad decisions. Our tongues should lead our bodies in the right direction.

To Speak With Wisdom

Fill in the blanks for the following verses, and answer the questions that follow.

1. Proverbs 10:31: "The _____ of the _____ brings forth _____, but the _____ _____ will be cut out."

Whose mouth brings forth wisdom?

What does it mean to be righteous?

2. Ecclesiastes 10:12: "The _____ of a _____ man's mouth are _____, but the _____ of a _____ shall _____ him up."

Think of someone you know who talks like a fool. How do people react when this person talks?

Think of someone you know who speaks with wisdom. How do people react when this person talks?

If we want to follow God's commands and do the right thing, then we must use wisdom for every decision about what to say and what not to say.

To Speak With Sincerity
Fill in the blanks for the following verses.

• Matthew 15:8-9: "These people draw near to Me with their
_____, and honor Me with their _____, but their
_____ is far from Me. And in vain they worship Me, teaching
as _____ the _____ of men."

Again, Jesus referred to the scribes and Pharisees in these verses. He knew they were only pretending to honor Him in order to make a good impression on others. Because their hearts were not genuine, their worship was not for Jesus but for their own personal motives. We also find the following in 1 Peter 3:10-11: "For He who would love life and see good days, let him refrain his tongue from evil, and his lips from speaking deceit. Let him turn away from evil and do good; let him seek peace and pursue it."

Don't be the kind of person who deceives others with her words; instead, be the kind of person whose words reflect her actions. If your actions are admirable, so too will be your words.

What do you think will happen if your actions are shameful, but you brag about what a great person you are?

_____

_____

Others will know very quickly when we are not being sincere. They will know us by our words and our actions, and they will know what our true intentions are.

To Speak With Respect
When I was in first grade, there was another Elizabeth in my class who was very different from me; she had the reputation of being bold, bossy and blunt. Although she was one of the shortest students in class, just about everyone was afraid of her. One day she suddenly disappeared from the class, and we heard it was because she called the teacher a

Profanity (noun): offensive language; an offensive word[11]

bad word. We were shocked. Once the initial shock finally wore off, however, our feelings changed to anger and disappointment that our peer had actually used such a terrible word to describe our beloved teacher.

Fill in the blanks for 1 John 4:4-6.

"You are of _____, little children, and have _____ them, because He who is in you is _____ than he who is in the _____. They are of the _____. Therefore they speak as of the _____, and the _____ hears them. We are of _____. He who knows _____ hears us; he who is not of _____ does not hear us. By this we know the spirit of _____ and the spirit of _____."

We already mentioned remaining silent as a way of respecting others; another way is to guard our mouths from bad language. When we use bad language, we do not speak as children of God, and we do not speak with a spirit of truth. By guarding our mouths, we acknowledge that such language is inappropriate and that it's not fair for others to hear it. We also set ourselves apart from the world as Jesus instructed in Matthew 5:14.

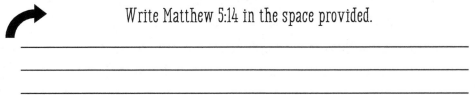

Write Matthew 5:14 in the space provided.

_____

_____

_____

Finally, we show respect to God by using only appropriate language.

God feels hurt when we use inappropriate words just as He felt with the Israelites in Ezekiel 36:20: "When they came to the nations, wherever they went, they profaned My holy name – when they said of them, 'These are the people of the LORD, and yet they have gone out of His land.' " Even though the Israelites did not use curse words, they profaned the Lord's name by disrespecting Him.

Exodus 20:7 tells us that "the LORD will not hold him guiltless who takes His name in vain." How would you feel if others yelled your name in anger every time something bad happened as if you were the one to blame? That's exactly how God feels when we take His name in vain; we give His name a negative connotation instead of a positive one. These profane words are part of what we will have to give account for on the day of judgment. So rather than using His name negatively, we should praise and exalt it.

Speak the Words of Christ

One of the best ways to learn to speak with purity is to follow Christ's example. According to 1 Peter 2:22, no deceit was found in His mouth. We also find that "when He was reviled, [He] did not revile in return; when He suffered, He did not threaten, but committed Himself to Him who judges righteously" (v. 23). Even when others beat Him, spat upon Him, and led Him to the cruel cross, He never once used His tongue inappropriately. He was probably angry at the others, but He did not use His tongue as a means of lashing out against them or calling attention to Himself. His example proves that no matter how difficult the situation, we can always control our tongues and speak with purity.

In John 7, Jesus explained that many who heard Him instantly believed in Him – just because of the way He spoke. Later, when the chief priests and Pharisees asked why no one had brought Jesus, the officers answered, "No man ever spoke like this Man!" (v. 46). When you talk, do others notice a difference? Can they see that you set yourself apart and try to be a positive influence on others with your words? Or do they think you talk no differently from any other girl your age?

> *"A clean heart won't let your mouth speak dirty. Purify your heart, and you cleanse your speech." – Unknown*

A Time to Imitate Christ

What would people say about you just by hearing you talk? Would they say you're a Christian and you want to please God? Or would they say you speak like a hypocrite, pretending to follow God but letting your mouth lead you in another direction?

In Colossians 3:8, we find some examples of "impurities" that come out of our mouths: "But now you yourselves are to put off all these: anger, wrath, malice, blasphemy, filthy language out of your mouth."

What impurities do you need to get out of your mouth?

_____

_____

> What are three steps you can take to have a purer mouth?

1. _____
2. _____
3. _____

In the movie *A Christmas Story*, Ralphie had to keep a bar of soap in his mouth for several minutes after his parents heard him say a bad word. Naturally the soap tasted so bad that he cried and thought, "I will never say that word again!" The way Ralphie felt about the soap is exactly how we should feel about any impurities that come out of our mouths – whether they be gossip, lies or profanity. We should want to spit them out as soon as they hit our tongues.

By controlling our tongues and speaking from the heart with purity, wisdom and sincerity, others will see that we are Christians in all that we do – including our attitudes. Philippians 4:8 says, "Finally, brethren, whatever things are true, whatever things are noble, whatever things are just, whatever things are pure, whatever things are lovely, whatever things are of good report, if there is any virtue and if there is anything praiseworthy – meditate on these things."

Remember the example of the sweet and salty water from the introduction? Anything that is not true, noble, just or pure as mentioned in the verses above, is not sweet or even healthy to drink. It is warm, polluted and bitter, and the longer it stays in our mouth, the more disgusting it will become. Let's promise to make every effort to recognize these impurities on our tongues and remove them as soon as possible, before they can harm us or others. Let's promise to fill our mouths with the rich desserts found in God's Word. Let's promise to encourage others, confess our faults, give thanks, and spread the good news rather than gossip, lie, criticize or disrespect others. Most importantly, let's promise to imitate Christ with every word we utter, striving to set a positive example with our speech that no one – even God – should feel ashamed of. I hope that you have been edified by reading this book as much as I have been by writing it.

Read the sentences and scriptures below, and decide whether you agree or disagree with the statement.

- The tongue can be tamed (see James 3:2, 8). _____
- We stumble in many ways with what we say (see James 3:2). _____

- A fountain can give bitter and fresh water at the same time (see James 3:11). _____

  - A small flame can cause an entire forest to burn down (see James 3:5). _____

Practice What You Speak

Individual Challenge: Undefiled Entertainment

 ## Purpose:

To eliminate gradually the sources of profanity in our day-to-day lives.

 ## Instructions:

While it is true that the words that come out of our mouths are what defile us, the more we hear bad language, the more likely we are to repeat it. And although we can't always control what the people around us say, we can try to listen to profanity as little as possible. To do so, challenge yourself to listen only to music that will not defile you. (This doesn't mean you have to listen to hymns all day, but you should choose your music more carefully.) Do the same thing with the movies and TV shows you watch. Challenge yourself to go a week, then a month, then six months, and then a year without listening to profane music or watching profane movies and shows.

Group Activity: Candy Tasting

 ## Purpose:

To realize that others will know us more by the tasteful words emanating from our mouths than by the label we give ourselves.

 ## Instructions:

The teacher or class leader should bring a bag of Jolly Ranchers to class. The girls should close their eyes, put a piece of candy in their mouths, and see if they can guess the flavor. Just as we can usually tell what kind of candy we're eating without reading the label, others will quickly know what kind of person we are by the words we use – whether bitter, salty or sweet.

 # Optional:

The teacher or class leader can bring each girl the following candies as reminders of how they should use their tongues.

• *Jolly Ranchers* – be jolly or encouraging with your words.

• *Starbursts* – be evangelistic, "bursting" to tell others about Jesus.

• *Reese's Peanut Butter Cups* – be silent and listen more often (it's hard to talk with peanut butter sticking to your mouth).

• *Hershey's Milk Chocolate* – be rich and pure with your words.

Endnotes

1 See http://www.merriam-webster.com/dictionary/edify.

2 See http://www.dummies.com/how-to/content/greeting-and-saying-goodbye-in-hebrew.html.

3 See http://www.merriam-webster.com/dictionary/sincere.

4 These questions were adapted from http://www.kidssundayschool.com/324/gradeschool/sin-revealed.php.

5 See http://www.merriam-webster.com/dictionary/responsibility.

6 See http://www.pureheartvision.org/resources/docs/yeakley/Good%20News%20and%20Bad%20News_A%20Realistic%20Assessment%20of%20Churchs%20of%20Christ%20in%20the%20USA.pdf.

7 See http://www.merriam-webster.com/dictionary/deceit.

8 See http://www.merriam-webster.com/dictionary/submit.

9 See http://www.merriam-webster.com/dictionary/humility.

10 This lesson was adapted from http://www.preaching.com/sermons/11563583/.

11 See http://www.merriam-webster.com/dictionary/profanity.

Printed in the USA
CPSIA information can be obtained
at www.ICGtesting.com
LVHW022156021023
759954LV00035B/667